# Grandpa Saw
# The Light

*A Partial Autobiography by*

DR. MIKE DUFFY

ISBN 979-8-89130-718-6 (paperback)
ISBN 979-8-89043-426-5 (digital)

Christian Faith Publishing
832 Park Avenue
Meadville, PA 16335
www.christianfaithpublishing.com

Printed in the United States of America

# Why This Book?

I have lived for nearly three-quarters of a century on planet Earth! I was born in America and have lived here my entire life. I have had the privilege of visiting forty-nine of the fifty states. I have visited other countries and have experienced and appreciated their cultures, including Bermuda, Canada, Finland, Germany, Guam, Japan, Mexico, Russia/Soviet Union, Ukraine, and Vietnam. I have enjoyed golf games on some of the most famous courses in the world, Pebble Beach, Spyglass, Whistling Straits, the Ocean Course at Kiawah Island, the Olympic Club and Harding Park in San Francisco, Royal Ka'anapoli on the island of Maui, TPC Sawgrass, PGA National in Palm Beach, and many others. I have been fishing on some of the greatest fisheries in the world with my kids and grandkids and have witnessed the majesty and extraordinary beauty of the great outdoors of God's creation. My preaching/teaching ministry has taken me to several hundred different churches, many Christian camps, colleges, universities, and countries.

During my life, I have experienced good times and bad times. I have lived in extreme poverty and with extraordinary wealth. I have seen some ugly parts of life and some beautiful parts too. I have lived through the horrors of war and the tragedies of death. I have suffered pain and loss and healing and gain. I have experienced heartache and heartbreak. I have experienced joy and rejoicing that are beyond words. I have been influenced by some wonderful people and I have been able to influence others and I have been rejected by some. I have started businesses and closed businesses, and the list could go on and on. The point is this: in spite of the difficulties, I consider myself to have lived a rich, full life!

At the time of this writing, I have been married to my wife, Geri, for fifty-six years. God blessed us with three children, twelve grandchildren, and four great-grandchildren. We are engaged in a wonderful church and live in a nice community.

I find myself in retirement these days with quite a bit of time on my hands. Through nearly forty years of executive leadership, where time and energy were often scarce commodities, I have accumulated a vast amount of experience, including teaching, counseling, and public speaking. I have been involved in developing strategies and executing operational plans. I have a large library of original articles, sermons, study notes, and a well-used thought tank where I have recorded a wealth of wisdom.

My first desire in writing this book is to share with my family—my kids, grandkids, and great-grandkids—some of these resources and some of the events of my life that I believe have some relevance for them so they have a fuller understanding of their own lives. As time goes by, some of what I have to tell them now will be comforting or more precious to them later. My hope, too, is that each will see that they, in their own unique way, have been a source of great joy and blessing to me.

I also hope this book will be a source of encouragement to many so they share their own story with others, particularly their loved ones. Everyone's life is a unique story, and it is meant to be shared with others. Some stories are more dramatic or sensational than others, but all are important.

Your story is about God's work in your life and your response to Him. I hope this book is a source of blessing for you.

# Grandpa Saw the Light

Grandpa saw the light by the mercy and grace of God.

## Living in Darkness

It is fascinating to me how our eyes adjust to the darkness. Once the lights go out, in just a brief time, we are able to see just enough to maneuver through the dark. This only happens because there is a source of light somewhere within our purview. It just is not close or immediately obvious. It may be a few stars on a night when the moon is not visible. It could be the glimmer from a little nightlight in an adjacent room. It might be the glow of the lights of a distant city reflecting off the bottoms of some overhanging clouds. Somewhere there is just enough light to accommodate the adjustment.

In contrast, when I think about absolute darkness, my mind goes back to the experience our family had on a tour through Mammoth Cave in Kentucky. Early in the tour, everyone in our group was standing in a large room. The guide referred to the room as The Dome Room. He was explaining the history of the caves, including their use during the Civil War, and some of the unique features we were about to see. At one point, he told everyone to stand still and perhaps take the hand of the person next to them because in a few seconds the lights were going to be turned off. We were about to experience total darkness.

When the lights went out, it got dark, very dark! And after a few seconds, no adjustment! Wow, that was a new experience! I waved my hand in front of my face, close enough to feel the wind as it passed by, but I could see nothing. No shadow. Not even a slight difference in the density of the darkness. It was dark!

I have often thought of that cave tour when reading my Bible and coming to passages that speak of mankind living in darkness. The darkness is the result of sin.

## Adam Did It

The Bible teaches us that it was Adam's sin that plunged the entire human race into darkness. The Apostle Paul wrote in his letter to the believers in Rome an explanation of this predicament. He said, "Wherefore, as by one man sin entered into the world, and death by sin; and so death passed upon all men, for that all have sinned" (Romans 5:12). When Adam disobeyed God in the Garden of Eden, it plunged the entire human race into sin. Adam was exiled from the presence of God. He would no longer be with the Light but would live in spiritual darkness.

The Bible often depicts man as being blind because of sin. Perhaps a good illustration of the darkness in which lost sinners live is given by Paul in his defense as he was on trial before King Agrippa. Paul was testifying of his own conversion to Christ when he shared this account:

> And I said, Who art thou, Lord? And he said, I am Jesus whom thou persecutest. But rise, and stand upon thy feet: for I have appeared unto thee for this purpose, to make thee a minister and a witness both of these things which thou hast seen, and of those things in the which I will appear unto thee; delivering thee from the people, and from the Gentiles, unto whom now I send thee, to open their eyes, *and to turn them from darkness to light, and from the power of Satan*

*unto God,* that they may receive forgiveness of sins, and inheritance among them which are sanctified by faith that is in me. (Acts 26:15–18; emphasis added)

God intended to save Paul and then use Paul as a minister to carry the light of the Gospel to the Gentile world. Up until this time, the Gospel was being preached primarily to the Jewish world. But because of the Jew's rejection of Jesus, God opened the door of salvation to the Gentiles too. Those who would believe the Gospel and receive Christ were characterized as having turned from the darkness of sin to the light of salvation, escaping the clutches of Satan, receiving God's forgiveness, being reconciled to God and adopted into God's family.

Since Adam, every man is born of the seed of man and, thus, is born with a sinful nature. That means he has a tendency or bent toward sin. From Adam and down through every generation since, man is born with this curse. The sinful nature is so easy to see in our world. Just put a couple of toddlers together in a room with some toys. Before long, you will see the selfish, sinful nature interrupt that budding relationship. "That's mine!" and "I want what's mine!" The two might even get physical! You have seen it, right?

Oh, and by the way, this is why it was necessary for Jesus to be born of a virgin. He was not born of the seed of the man but was conceived by the Holy Spirit, and thus it was possible for Him to live a sinless life and be the satisfactory substitute in paying the death penalty for sin on our behalf. Thank you, Lord!

Jesus said men love to live in darkness. They believe that darkness conceals their evil behavior, and they do not want their sin exposed and reproved, so they operate in darkness whenever possible. Here is what he said:

*He that believeth on him is not condemned: but he that believeth not is condemned already, because he hath not believed in the name of the only begotten Son of God. And this is the condemnation,*

3

*that light is come into the world, and men loved
darkness rather than light, because their deeds were
evil. For everyone that doeth evil hateth the light,
neither cometh to the light, lest his deeds should
be reproved. But he that doeth truth cometh to the
light, that his deeds may be made manifest, that
they are wrought in God.* (John 3:18–21)

Have you ever considered how much late-night activity involves evil behavior? Think about it! There is a reason for this, and Jesus just told us what the reason is. Sinful men with sinful natures love sin. However, the shame that accompanies sin, because of the God-given conscience man possesses, causes them to want to hide their sin. Is it not true that we all experience this? You know, "When the cat is away, the mice will play!" However cute this saying may be, the truth of it condemns us all. I remember reading a clever little saying that I have used on occasion that illustrates our sinfulness. It says, "He that lieth down with dogs shall rise up with fleas!" How true!

Another solemn truth from this passage is this: man is already condemned. Because of his sin nature, he sins. And because he is already a sinner, he is condemned. One might ask, "What does a person have to do in order to go to hell?" The answer is, "Nothing, he is already headed that way." He is condemned already. He must do something to go to heaven, and that is to repent and believe what God said and receive Jesus Christ as his Savior. That is a personal decision each one has to make for themselves. No one can make it for another, and no one is born with a ticket already punched for heaven. They must make the decision to receive the gift God is providing.

## Our Conscience Gets "Seared"

The secret to cooking a good steak is to get a nice sear on both sides of the piece of meat. Once the sear is there, the juices are sealed inside. As a result, the meat is more tender and flavorful when it is cooked. Searing creates a barrier.

The constant practice of sin eventually "sears" our conscience. When that happens, we have become desensitized to sin. Or should we say, sin was normalized as acceptable behavior in our conscience even though God says it is wrong. One with a seared conscience has moved, and continues to move, away from God.

> *Now the Spirit speaketh expressly, that in the latter times some shall depart from the faith, giving heed to seducing spirits, and doctrines of devils; Speaking lies in hypocrisy; **having their conscience seared with a hot iron;** Forbidding to marry, and commanding to abstain from meats, which God hath created to be received with thanksgiving of them which believe and know the truth. For every creature of God is good, and nothing to be refused, if it be received with thanksgiving: For it is sanctified by the word of God and prayer.* (1 Timothy 4:1–5)

Before long, they not only shamelessly indulge in sinful behavior but also think everyone should also indulge. There is no longer any consideration given to God and God's Word (see Romans 1:28–32 for an example of this).

I can surely attest to man's love for darkness. With very little exposure to the Light when I was growing up, sin did not appear sinful to me.

## Exposure Without Recognition

I suspect there were many times where I was exposed to the light of the Gospel of Jesus Christ, but I did not recognize what it was. Is this a problem? Or is it part of God's process? I think the answer to both questions is "Yes!" It was a problem for me, but it was also part of a process God was using in my life.

Exposure without recognition is a problem. Recognizing the Gospel as the only solution to man's real problem is vital to one's life on planet Earth now and ultimately his everlasting destiny, either with or away from God.

Some of those exposures to the Gospel I now recognize in my life include the following:

- *An exposure through religion where the blind may have been leading the blind*

  I first learned of Jesus's death on the cross at a Catholic Catechism class in Lee, Illinois. My parents sent my two brothers and me to these classes. My older brother, Steve, was also serving there as an altar boy. I was in first or second grade. The nuns who were teaching the classes were serving in that diocese, and conducting these classes was part of their work. They were pretty much teaching from a "historical" and a "religious" perspective. I understood intellectually that Jesus was crucified, dying on the cross, but did not grasp its true relational significance.

  I will assume their intentions were good, but I suspect now we were sent there by our folks because my father's mother in New York was a devout Catholic. She may have exercised some influence on Dad. Mom's family, who lived nearby, were Lutherans who attended a rural church a few miles outside of Lee. I do not remember them making any effort to teach us boys about that religion.

- *The 10 Commandments*

  When I was growing up, the posting of the Ten Commandments was commonplace. They were posted in the public schools, the government offices, many of the businesses in town, and of course, they we on display at churches both inside and outside. I considered them to be a set of moral rules man was to follow. I think most people viewed them like that. It is so sad and tragic to see them absent from the public forum in our day.

  The Ten Commandments are often referred to as the Law of Moses. They are part of the Law of Moses but not the entire law. God gave the Ten Commandments to Moses on Mount Sinai to give to the people of Israel as they journeyed toward the Promised Land, but there were other mandates and practices in the Law of Moses too.

The Apostle Paul, writing to the churches of Galatia, revealed the ultimate purpose of the commandments when he said, "Wherefore the law was our schoolmaster **to bring us unto Christ,** that we might be justified by faith" (Galatians 3:24).

Exposure to the Ten Commandments confronts our conscience with the understanding that we have failed to live up to God's perfect standard. The Bible declares that "all have sinned." And now we stand guilty before God, unable to save ourselves from our own sin. And so with this understanding, we look for someone who can save us, someone whose sacrificial death was sufficient to satisfy the righteous demands of the holiness of God. A search of God's truth, the Scriptures, tells us there is only one who can meet the demands, and that is Jesus. "For there is one God, and one mediator between God and men, the man Christ Jesus; Who gave himself a ransom for all, to be testified in due time" (1 Timothy 2:5–6). I saw the Ten Commandments on many occasions, but I did not recognize their true purpose or their importance to me personally. The one thing that was always obvious to me was this—I was not keeping all the commandments!

• *We called him Deacon.*

Another significant exposure came when we lived in Kirkland, Illinois. I was in fifth grade when we moved to Kirkland. My folks had purchased a business, a tavern named The Farmers Inn. It was one of three taverns in Kirkland.

We had a great neighborhood of kids in Kirkland. We would often get together for afternoon or evening games of kick the can or hide-and-seek. It was not unusual to have twenty-five or thirty kids playing at the same time. During the summer days, we would play baseball, sometimes just a game called work-up if we only had a handful of kids, or a full-blown game if we had enough for two teams. Other times it would be a game of basketball on the impressive outdoor court Mr. Thurlby made for his kids.

One family in the neighborhood stood out as "being a little different" from most of the other kids and their families, the Knauss family. The son, Donny, was called by most of us Deacon. I really did not understand why or what the significance of that name was.

The most significant memory I have of this family was the converted camper-trailer that was parked in their yard. It was red and cream-colored and sported the attractively printed name "Miniature Land" on both sides. Donny's dad, Stan Knauss, had created a model community and circus and displayed it in the trailer. He was a real artist. The buildings were made of balsa wood, and everything was made to scale. It really was a tremendous exhibit. He showed it at fairs, community events, and who knows where else.

I would later find out that Donny's family were born-again, Bible-believing Christians. I would even preach many years later in the church they had attended in Rockford, Illinois, back then. Once again, I had been exposed to the light but did not recognize it. However, God did! He was at work.

- *Why did I buy that Bible?*

What was happening and why, I did not know. This time, the exposure came at a transition and change in my life. I was nineteen, and my new bride, Geri, was eighteen when we eloped and "tied the knot" at the courthouse in Sycamore, Illinois. We moved into our first apartment; it was the upstairs of an older house in Hampshire, Illinois. It was convenient, as we both worked at the toy factory in town. It was a division of Milton Bradley where some of the Fisher-Price toys were made.

Just a few weeks after being married in early December, Geri dropped me off at work a little after 4:00 p.m. My regular shift was from 4:30 p.m. to 5:00 a.m., four days a week. On this particular day, she showed back up at break time a couple of hours later, tears in her eyes and carrying a piece of mail. It was my draft notice. I would be entering the US Army in just a few months, April 1968.

My training would take place at Fort Polk, Louisiana. I went through Basic Training (eight weeks), Leadership Preparation Course (two weeks), and Advanced Infantry Training (eight weeks) in succession. Upon completion of these trainings, I was without orders for what would be next. They sent me on "30-day leave" and then had me report back to Fort Polk to serve in administration as "permanent party." Geri accompanied me when I returned to Fort Polk. All told, I was at Fort Polk for just over a year.

And then in the spring of 1969, I got orders to go to Vietnam. The Tet Offensive had just happened, and the war was at its zenith. Back home, the protests were raging, and our country was greatly divided.

Geri was "very pregnant" when we left Louisiana for Illinois to get her settled into an apartment near her parents before I left for the war. Our first child, Mick, was born just a few days before I reported for duty in Oakland, California, en route to Vietnam. Our flight overseas included refueling stops in Hawaii and Guam before landing at Bien Hoa Air Base, South Vietnam. Many times on this journey my thoughts took me to some dark places. I was quite sure that I had seen Geri, Mick, and the rest of the family for the last time. My expectation of surviving the war was low. One of my classmates, Jack Vowles, had already been killed over there.

Somewhere during this journey, and I really have no idea today where it happened, I was exposed to the light again. I do not remember the context or the pitch, but somehow I ended up ordering a huge family Bible, having it sent directly to Geri. Why I did this is still a mystery to me. Someone had to have said something for me to make this purchase through the PX. Exposure again but no recognition.

- *Good for them but not for me!*
  I returned home from Vietnam on a Friday in December of 1969 and started working at Data Documents, Inc. in Genoa, Illinois, on the following Monday. I was the company's new office manager. My brother-in-law Jim was instrumental in me getting the job. Anyway, it was the beginning of a career in the computer supplies industry that would last fourteen years—from an office manager to administrative manager and then into sales. The career would include living in Genoa, Illinois; Omaha, Nebraska; North Madison, Connecticut; Auburn, Illinois; and, finally, Normal, Illinois.

  While living in Omaha, I was busy climbing the corporate ladder. Our family grew with the addition of two daughters, Michelle and Kelly. It was during this time that a dear lady brought the Gospel of Jesus Christ to my wife and our next-door neighbor, Jane. Geri was saved and began attending a little Baptist church down the street. I remember going to her baptism there. Another exposure! But no recognition! I was too busy with my career, with making money. I thought the church was good for my family but not for me!

- *Accelerated exposure*
  The exposure continued with greater frequency now that Geri and the kids were faithful in church. Even when I received a transfer to Connecticut, they continued. Geri joined a little church in Clinton, Connecticut. The pastor there taught her how to really study the Bible. I had the

Light living with me now! And it was shining. Geri was growing in her faith, and Mick had come to Christ for salvation under Geri's tutelage. Meanwhile, I was still serving my god, my idols—money and my career! But God was at work too! He was doing his "drawing" work in my heart. I just did not recognize it!

Our company went through a corporate acquisition, being purchased by the Pitney Bowes Corporation. Their home office was in Connecticut, about an hour from our plant. This resulted in their leadership spending much time at our facility and me getting a look at the "cruel underbelly" of the merger and acquisition realities in the corporate world. Good people lost their jobs! Friends' careers were cut off without warning! Nepotism was exposed to me as being customary practice, crushing the promise of climbing the corporate ladder. My idol was being shattered! The god of company loyalty was destroyed in my imagination. The confidence and the peace of the prospect of a long, stable, relationship with the company became as uncertain and unstable as a leaky ship on a stormy sea.

I asked for a change of venue! I wanted out of New England and to get back to the comfort and safety of my roots, the Midwest. I had a great history of success with our company, and so they facilitated my request. I would have to make a compromise, though. I had been in management for my entire career. I would now have to assume a role in sales. Although I had no experience in sales, I took their offer just to get close to familiar territory, and so we were off to Central Illinois. My sales career had begun.

Geri found a new church. Both of our daughters put their faith in Christ during this time, and Grandpa Duncan came and stayed with us for a while. He loved the Lord and was a kind old man. More exposure, no recognition! God's truth, however, was marching on!

In sales, I had success like I had never experienced it before! We were doing well financially. The growth in my territory brought opportunity. In year two as a salesperson, I earned a place on the company's annual sales trip. Geri and I went to the Acapulco Princess Resort in Acapulco, Mexico, with about fifty people from every division of our company, all expenses paid. This would become an annual gig as I achieved "President's Club" status, meaning my sales were among the top 5 percent internationally. We made additional trips with the company to the Hamilton Princess Hotel and Beach Resort in Bermuda known as the Pink Palace, the La Costa Resort and Spa near San Diego, California, and Ka'anapali Beach Club in Lahaina, Maui, Hawaii.

The growth in my sales territory brought another opportunity. Geographically my area to cover was most of Illinois south of Chicago to north of St. Louis. This meant a lot of driving and an occasional overnight in a hotel. I did not enjoy the traveling part. There were four key cities in which I focused my efforts, attempting to "skim the cream" and ultimately decide which part of my territory to split off to another salesperson. That would greatly reduce my traveling. There would be residual benefit to me financially by doing this too. To the north were the markets of Peoria, including the Caterpillar Corporation, and Bloomington/Normal where State Farm Insurance Company's world headquarters was located. To the south were Springfield, including the many government agencies of the State of Illinois, and Decatur, where A.E. Staley and Archer Daniels Midland's home offices were located. These were agricultural industry leaders.

Before long, it was obvious to me that geographically the northern portion held most promise. The company hired another salesperson and my family moved to Normal, Illinois. Little did I realize that God's drawing was intensified.

Geri and I bought a house in Normal in August of 1979. Just down the street was the elementary school where our kids would be enrolled that first fall. As school started,

Geri was outside one day and noticed a little boy playing across the street. She wondered why he was not in school. She asked and found out he went to a Christian school in Normal. Geri asked to meet his mother and soon found out she had a Christian neighbor right across the street from our house. She accepted Amy's invitation to church and visited Calvary Baptist Church the next Sunday. She loved the church and became a member. She and the kids attended every Sunday, including Sunday school. The Light was shining, and God was drawing!

In just a few short months, the kids' Christmas program at Calvary was my introduction to their church. I met their Pastor, Dr. Arno Q. Weniger, that morning in December. For the first time in my life, I was impressed with one of Geri's pastors. He did not seem to be the "country bumpkin" stereotype I had developed in my mind. He was a "three-piece suit" kind of guy who was friendly, articulate, and impressive to me. This mattered because in just a few weeks, he would visit our home, and I would welcome him instead of finding a reason not to be there. The light was shining again, and perhaps I was beginning to recognize it. About time, I guess, because as I would find out later, Geri and the kids had been praying for my salvation regularly.

- *From the insurance man to the assurance man!*

It was Monday night, January 21, 1980. I had an insurance salesman upstairs in our living room when the doorbell rang. It was Dr. Weniger. Geri let him in, and they went downstairs to our family room to wait for me to finish upstairs with the insurance man. As Dr. Weniger would later put it, I got rid of the "insurance man" to meet with the "assurance man"!

After the insurance man left, I went down to the family room. Dr. Weniger began asking me about my work and what I did. He patiently waited while I told him. After thanking me for sharing, he said, "Let me tell you what I

13

do." What could I say? He had listened to me. How could I refuse? So he told me. He then asked a question that, to my recollection, I had never been asked before. He said, "If you died today, are you sure you would go to heaven?" I quickly responded, "Yes!" I think both he and Geri were shocked to hear me say that. He followed the question up with another, "How do you know that?" I do not even remember if I had an answer to that question. I do know that I had no good reason to believe I would be in heaven! It just seemed like the right thing to say. After all, who would say no and then not be concerned enough about that to ask for help?

Dr. Weniger then asked me if anyone had ever shown me in the Bible what God had to say about the issue. Although some had undoubtedly tried before and I just did not recognize it, I said, "No." He asked if he could show me, to which I consented. As I recall, Dr. Weniger showed me of my need as a sinner from Romans chapters 3 and 6 and God's provision of the gift of salvation in chapter 6. The verse of scripture that I recall most, however, is 1 John 5:13, "These things have I written unto you that believe on the name of the Son of God: that ye may know that ye have eternal life, and that ye may believe on the name of the Son of God." God wants us to *know*! He wanted me to know, too!

# I Saw the Light!

I recognized my need as a lost sinner! I recognized God was offering a gift that I could not earn, did not deserve, or could not obtain for myself.

Asking if I would like to receive Christ as my Savior right now, we knelt together by our couch. He prayed, and then I prayed, confessing my need for salvation and my understanding and belief that Jesus had died on the cross for me. He paid my sin debt, death, so I could receive the gift of salvation God wanted to give me. I was saved by Christ alone, by grace alone, through faith alone! I now had a living relationship with God.

Today, I am secure in Jesus. The presence of the indwelling Holy Spirit of God is the "earnest of my inheritance." One day, God will complete the transaction, transporting me from mortality to immortality, and I will be with Him in heaven forever.

## The Problem for Those Who Do Not Recognize the Light

It is a problem for those who do not recognize the Gospel because of their current standing before God. They are "dead in trespasses and sin." Until they respond to the light of the Gospel, they remain in that condition. Jesus made this perfectly clear in John 3 when he said they were "condemned already." One could not be "more" condemned than he already is. He, as a condemned sinner, is lost in his sin and is currently en route to the great white throne judgment described at the end of Revelation chapter 20. There he will be judged for his sin and banished for all eternity from the presence of God. He will suffer the anguish of God's judgment in the lake of fire, a place where it is said, "The smoke of their torment will ascend upward forever and ever, and there will be no rest day or night" (Revelation 14:11). Could one face a bigger problem? I think not!

I know there are some who are of the persuasion that when they die, they just cease to exist. That is all there is! They are gone. I will be honest with you. If this were so, if this might be the way things would be, I would not have bothered to write this book because I could live with that! You know, live and let die! Game over! Oh well! But that is not reality!

And I also know there are many who believe they can do something to earn a spot in heaven or deserve a place there. Good works or deeds will settle their sin debt! In fact, almost every religion and religious cult on the planet believes this way. They believe it is about what they do, not what Jesus has done. To me, these people fall into one of two categories. Either they are ignorant of God's truth or they reject God's truth.

- *For the ignorant*

Let me encourage you to listen to what I have to say for a few minutes and then go to a Bible, perhaps your Bible, and verify what I am telling you. The Bible is emphatic and consistent with the message of salvation. And you need to believe God, not me! God's Word makes it clear in many passages, including:

*For by grace are ye saved through faith: and that not of yourselves: it is the gift of God: Not of works, lest any man should boast.* Ephesians 2:8-9

*I do not frustrate the grace of God: for if righteousness come by the law, then Christ is dead in vain.* (Galatians 2:21)

*But after that the kindness and love of God our Saviour toward man appeared, Not by works of righteousness which we have done, but according to his mercy he saved us, by the washing of regeneration, and renewing of the Holy Ghost; Which he shed on us abundantly through Jesus Christ our Saviour; That being justified by his grace, we should be made heirs according to the hope of eternal life.* (Titus 3:4–7)

*For there is one God, and one mediator between God and men, the man Christ Jesus...* (1 Timothy 2:5)

*For the wages of sin is death; but the gift of God is eternal life through Jesus Christ our Lord.* (Romans 6:23)

Salvation, which includes the forgiveness of sin, reconciliation to a living relationship with God, and everlasting life with God in heaven, is clearly a gift that God wants us to possess. All we have to do is accept this gift from Him by faith—that is, taking Him at His Word. It cannot be earned, or it would no longer be a gift. Instead, it would be compensation or a reward for something we did (i.e., good work or deeds)!

A person is not reconciled to God because they are good or do good things. They are reconciled because of God's love for them. The declared penalty for sin is death (Romans 6:23), not goodness and favor. The quality and quantity of good deeds does not meet the righteous demands of a holy God! Nice try but not enough!

Can you accept the fact that it is *grace*, not *goodness* that will satisfy God? Look again at Ephesians 2:8–9 as previously stated! It says it is by grace we are saved!

There is no reason to remain ignorant of what God has said. As difficult as you might think this truth is to grasp, just take God at His Word. That is what faith is— believing God and acting accordingly!

- *For the truth rejector*

  Perhaps the writer of the letter to the Hebrews said it best:

  *For if we sin willfully after that we have received the knowledge of the truth, there remaineth no more sacrifice for sins, But a certain fearful looking for of judgment and fiery indignation, which shall devour the adversaries. He that despised Moses' law died without mercy under two or three witnesses: Of how much sorer punishment, suppose ye, shall he be thought worthy, who hath trodden underfoot the Son of God, and hath counted the blood of the covenant, wherewith he was sanctified, an unholy thing, and hath done despite unto the Spirit of grace? For we know him that hath said,*

*Vengeance belongeth unto me, I will recompense, saith the Lord. And again, The Lord shall judge his people. It is a fearful thing to fall into the hands of the living God.* (Hebrews 10:26–31)

I remember reading a quote many years ago that says, "You can deny God, but you cannot escape Him!" As God is the creator and sustainer of everything, no man can infringe on the power and providence of God. He is the author and finisher of our faith, the Alpha and the Omega. One either believes God or pays the price of sin.

God has removed all excuses for mankind. Consider the Apostle Paul's writing to the believers in Rome. In the opening paragraphs of this lengthy letter, he wrote:

*For I am not ashamed of the gospel of Christ: for it is the power of God unto salvation to everyone that believeth; to the Jew first, and also to the Greek. For therein is the righteousness of God revealed from faith to faith: as it is written, The just shall live by faith.*

*For the wrath of God is revealed from heaven against all ungodliness and unrighteousness of men, who hold the truth in unrighteousness; Because that which may be known of God is manifest in them; for God hath shewed it unto them. For the invisible things of him from the creation of the world are clearly seen, being understood by the things that are made, even his eternal power and Godhead;* **so that they are without excuse:** *Because that, when they knew God, they glorified him not as God, neither were thankful; but became vain in their imaginations, and their foolish heart was darkened. Professing themselves to be wise, they became fools, And changed the glory of the uncorruptible God* *into an image made like to corruptible man, and to birds, and fourfooted beasts, and creeping things.*

*Wherefore God also gave them up to uncleanness through the lusts of their own hearts, to dishonour their own bodies between themselves: Who changed the truth of God into a lie, and worshipped and served the creature more than the Creator, who is blessed forever. Amen.*

*For this cause God gave them up unto vile affections: for even their women did change the natural use into that which is against nature: And likewise also the men, leaving the natural use of the woman, burned in their lust one toward another; men with men working that which is unseemly, and receiving in themselves that recompence of their error which was meet. And even as they did not like to retain God in their knowledge, God gave them over to a reprobate mind, to do those things which are not convenient; Being filled with all unrighteousness, fornication, wickedness, covetousness, maliciousness; full of envy, murder, debate, deceit, malignity; whisperers, Backbiters, haters of God, despiteful, proud, boasters, inventors of evil things, disobedient to parents, Without understanding, covenant breakers, without natural affection, implacable, unmerciful: Who knowing the judgment of God, that they which commit such things are worthy of death, not only do the same, but have pleasure in them that do them.* (Romans 1:16–32)

These are sobering words! Frightening if they are true too! And they are true. For the truth rejector, the consideration of these statements ought to at least cause one to say to himself, "What if they are true?" What is it that one would consider so valuable or precious that they would ignore or reject what God said? What thing, as the source

19

of temporal pleasure or vanishing importance, could possibly be worth the risk? How could one be so arrogant that they would consider their own belief more dependable than that of the proven Word of God? Where would such false confidence find its roots?

Much more could be written in this section about the consequence of rejection. Instead of wasting the time of the reader who might continue to reject God, let me offer this final word of encouragement: find out for yourself! Put God and His Word to the test! God loves you so much He is willing to accept the challenge. In the prophet Malachi's writing, God told the audience to put Him to the test, to prove Him: "Bring ye all the tithes into the storehouse, that there may be meat in mine house, and **prove me now herewith**, saith the LORD of hosts, if I will not open you the windows of heaven, and pour you out a blessing, that there shall not be room enough to receive it" (Malachi 3:10). Understanding the possible consequence of rejection, would this not be a worthwhile investment of your time, just to be sure?

And notice what God said in the Romans 1 passage about the heart of this matter. The heart was "foolish." Only a fool could ignore the overwhelming evidence of creation. They rejected God in their arrogance and ingratitude and professed themselves to be wise. Self-exaltation never produces good, stable outcomes. Refusing to be accountable to God, they sought to pervert the ways of God and to minimize Him into a religion or idol they could bring out or call upon when they chose to do so. They embraced a lie and rejected the truth, and that determined who they would serve! How sad! Their decision would bring a lifetime of trouble and an everlasting time of torment. Rejection has a price that is higher than anyone really wants to pay. Perhaps a little honesty and forethought would have changed their mind.

## The Process of God

Or as we suggested, is this part of God's process? Jesus said, "No man can come to me, except the Father which hath sent me draw him: and I will raise him up at the last day" (John 6:44).

In this passage, Jesus had just told a group of people in Capernaum who were following him, curious people who believed in God's existence and desired to do the works of God, that their job was "to believe on him whom he [God] had sent." He was speaking of himself. The people immediately asked Jesus to show them a sign so they could believe. They told Jesus that God had given their forefathers manna in the wilderness. Upon telling them this about their forefathers, Jesus told them he was the "bread of God" for them. It was God's will that "everyone which seeth the Son, and believeth on him, may have everlasting life" (John 6:40). This confused the crowd, and they began murmuring at Jesus—that is, they grumbled in skepticism and uncertainty, rejecting Jesus's claim to be the Bread of Life.

Then Jesus declared the process of God. In John 6:44, Jesus said no man would believe in him unless God was "drawing" them. If God did not draw, man would not believe. This word draw speaks of an inward power of attraction. It was God working on man's heart. He was showing man the "light of life" (John 8:12). The purpose of this was to bring man to a point of believing, and receiving for himself, the atoning work of Jesus. If they received Jesus as the Savior, their Savior, God would save them to everlasting life. Jesus had clearly stated this just a couple chapters earlier, "Verily, verily, I say unto you, He that heareth my word, and believeth on him that sent me, hath everlasting life, and shall not come into condemnation; but is passed from death unto life..." (John 5:24).

Jesus made the point again in John chapter 12, "And I, if I be lifted up from the earth, will draw all men unto me" (John 12:32).

The point is this: from the Garden of Eden, when the first man sinned in unbelief and disobedience, to this present moment, I think it would be accurate to say that God has been working His process. It is the process of reconciling mankind to Himself. Sin had separated man from the presence of, and fellowship with, God, whose primary characteristic is holiness or separateness. Sin cannot be in His presence.

From man's perspective, God has drawn him to a particular place at a particular time for a particular opportunity. He has prepared man's heart. He has organized the circumstance. He has sent His messenger with the truth. His Holy Spirit has approached this spiritually dead soul and shined the light of the Gospel in his heart, illuminating the truth, convicting him of his sinful life and the need of reconciliation. And if man, with a spirit of repentance, believes and receives the gift God is offering him, the transaction is made. The Spirit of God quickens the man, moving him from spiritual death to new life in Christ, sealing his salvation for the rest of eternity. Now being born again, the man's guilt is lifted, and the peace of God enters in. The man has been redeemed! *He saw the light, and it is now shining brightly in his own life!*

# Grandpa Shined the Light

*Grandpa shined the light* by living it. Not by being perfect but by making much progress in the process God had chosen by being willing and faithful.

## A Lifetime of Change

At the time of this writing, the author has been a follower of Jesus Christ for more than forty years. From that January evening in 1980 until now, God has had him on a journey, a journey of change. While change is considered hard by many, it is God's plan for those He saves. They have been saved from the penalty of their sin, which is death, separation from God. The Bible teaches us that lost people are physically alive but spiritually dead, separated from any relationship with God. Practically speaking, lost people just do not understand the things of God.

But once saved, not only are they saved from the penalty of sin, but they are also set free from the power of sin. Sin no longer has to be their slave master. By the grace and power of God, they can live a righteous life, learning and fulfilling God's will for their lives. The Apostle Paul wrote of this process in his letter to the Roman believers:

*And we know that all things work together for good to them that love God, to them who are the called according to his purpose. For whom he did*

*foreknow, he also did predestinate to be conformed
to the image of his Son, that he might be the first-
born among many brethren. Moreover whom he
did predestinate, them he also called: and whom he
called, them he also justified: and whom he justified, them he also glorified.* (Romans 8:28–30)

From the very beginning of human history, it was God's inten-
tion to save man from his sinful ways and then change him back into
what God had originally designed him to be.

Later in his letter, Paul encouraged these believers to embrace
God's process of change. It would be the "reasonable thing" to do
now that they were spiritually alive.

*I beseech you therefore, brethren, by the mercies
of God, that ye present your bodies a living sacrifice,
holy, acceptable unto God, which is your reasonable
service. And be not conformed to this world: but be
ye transformed by the renewing of your mind, that
ye may prove what is that good, and acceptable, and
perfect, will of God.* (Romans 12:1–2)

They were to approach life with the spirit of surrender and
submission to God, desiring to serve and please Him. They were to
renew their mind—that is, they were to learn and apply the truth
from God's Word that would teach them how they should live. When
they did so, they would understand and experience God's will.

Paul would also write of this change process to the church at
Ephesus. He exhorted them also to embrace the process of change.

*But ye have not so learned Christ; If so be
that ye have heard him, and have been taught by
him, as the truth is in Jesus: That ye put off con-
cerning the former conversation the old man, which
is corrupt according to the deceitful lusts; And be
renewed in the spirit of your mind; And that ye*

*put on the new man, which after God is created in righteousness and true holiness. Wherefore putting away lying, speak every man truth with his neighbour: for we are members one of another. Be ye angry, and sin not: let not the sun go down upon your wrath: Neither give place to the devil. Let him that stole steal no more: but rather let him labour, working with his hands the thing which is good, that he may have to give to him that needeth. Let no corrupt communication proceed out of your mouth, but that which is good to the use of edifying, that it may minister grace unto the hearers. And grieve not the holy Spirit of God, whereby ye are sealed unto the day of redemption. Let all bitterness, and wrath, and anger, and clamour, and evil speaking, be put away from you, with all malice: And be ye kind one to another, tenderhearted, forgiving one another, even as God for Christ's sake hath forgiven you.* (Ephesians 4:20–32)

Since they were now saved and learning the truth of Jesus and His Word, they were to "put away" their old, ungodly ways of living. They were to get their "attitude and understanding renovated" as they learned God's Word. Then they were to "put on" or put to practice what God was teaching them. It was in this fashion that God was recreating them in righteousness and true holiness. I summarize this process as "putting off, being renewed, and putting on." This is what should be happening regularly in my life as I grow in the grace and knowledge of the Lord. By the way, this is a great process for recognizing God's work in your life regularly. It is an incredible faith-building process too.

## Spiritual Nourishment for Living

Once I put my faith in Christ for my salvation, a new hunger for truth developed in my heart. The "light" had come on, and like a newborn baby desires its mother's milk, I now wanted more. Going to church that first Sunday after being saved was a new experience for me. I no longer felt out of place. The people did not seem to be a threat to me. The music, although different from what I had listened to my whole life, was truly a blessing. It delivered messages of hope, encouragement, and peace. Although the quality of the music was great, the content was even greater! What the preacher had to say made sense too. It seemed he knew exactly what I needed to hear! And it was like that week after week. I was developing an insatiable appetite for spiritual food. I even had the TV in the bedroom tuned in to *The Old-Time Gospel Hour* as I was getting dressed for church so I could listen to the preacher. I was hungry for truth!

For the first couple months after my salvation, we attended church every Sunday. And then one week, the church had a week-long revival/evangelistic meeting. Dr. Bill Rice III came to preach each service. His first message of the series that started on Sunday morning hit home for me. It was titled "Do Right!" Geri had served in the nursery that morning, and on the way home, she asked if we could come back for the evening service since she did not get to hear Dr. Rice's message. I was quick to agree, and so we returned for the evening service. God knew what we needed, and the hunger in my life was intensifying. We ended up going back each night that week.

## My First Prayer Breakfast

I even went to the Saturday morning men's prayer breakfast at the end of the week. This was a first-time experience for me. Dr. Bill was speaking there too. Even though I had no idea what a prayer breakfast was like, I went to hear him. In my imagination, I thought the guys would all eat together, and someone would begin the meal with a prayer. That was it! Sounded simple enough to me. There were forty to fifty men who showed up at seven that Saturday morning. Dr. Rice brought a short devotion from the Bible. Then the man who was leading the event, Roger Vawter, asked if there were any prayer requests. Many of the men responded with requests that were very personal and seemingly especially important to them. Then Roger excused us to break up into small groups and go somewhere in the building and pray together. Wow! I had never done that before! I had no idea what that would be like either.

Several of us men ended up in a room off to the side of the front foyer. There was a long, single pew on one wall of the room. All the men knelt down at the pew. I was on one end next to an exceptionally large black man who had played football at Illinois State University. His name was Jesse. Then from the other end of the line of men, someone started praying. Out loud! I think my blood pressure must have elevated fifty points, and my breathing quickened when I heard that. When he finished, the next man in line prayed and and then the next. They were headed in my direction. Yikes! Jesse must have sensed my nervousness and reached over and gently grabbed my arm. I looked at him, and he was looking at me. He quietly said, "Don't worry, Mike, just talk to God about what is on your heart." In a few minutes, Jesse took his turn praying, and when he ended, I began to talk to God! Amazing! Utterly amazing!

Prayer breakfast would become a priority for me and one of my favorite times of the week. New friendships began and quickly deepened as we shared and prayed together. I would later find out that this group of men had prayed for my salvation since my wife had joined the church in the fall of the previous year. What a special group of men they were to me.

# Feasting on the Word

Dr. Rice had his messages from our meeting and other meetings he had conducted, recorded, and duplicated on cassette tapes. At the end of the week, I purchased a copy of every message he had. I listened to them over and over as I traveled for work. Instead of music, I would just play tape after tape of Bible preaching. I was so hungry for the Word!

Other evangelists would come to Calvary the next couple of years too. Dr. Ron Comfort and Dr. Bill Hall became favorites, and many years later, both became friends. I bought all of their tapes too. The preaching of these three men plus a steady diet of preaching from

Pastor Weniger helped shape my spiritual life. To this day, I am so grateful to God for bringing them into my life. Praise the Lord for men like this, men who love the Lord and are faithful to preach His Word.

Somewhere along the way, I learned about Liberty Home Bible Institute. It was a correspondence course from Liberty University in Lynchburg, Virginia. It may have been advertised on *The Old-Time Gospel Hour*, or Dr. Weniger may have suggested it to me. In either case, I enrolled and got the tapes and books. I would study after work and on weekends. The content was solid and was helping me to "renew my mind." The Lord knows it needed a major renovation!

I do remember there were many times I felt so inadequate. It seemed like the more I learned, the less I knew. Really, it was just that I was learning that there was so much more to learn. My wife and children had all been saved before me and in church on a regular basis. They knew a lot of Bible! I thought I had a lot of catching up to do. This feeling of inadequacy no doubt contributed to my failure to be consistent in leading family devotions.

## Serving the Lord at Church

Geri and I both got busy serving in church. She already served in the nursery program. I became an usher. At the time, it was a huge step for me and a great blessing. I was in a rotation that served for a month every few months. I was at work for God! That was amazing to me. This kind of service was really important. It became a place to demonstrate faithfulness, a very important issue in discipleship.

We also started helping the youth pastor as lay-helpers to both the junior high and senior high youth groups. Our son had just become part of the junior high group. Our interest in what he was learning and doing resulted in the youth pastor asking us to serve as helpers in these ministries. It was a real blessing to help. And the growth it stimulated in us was tremendous. We got to hear the youth pastor preach to the kids at all of the activities. Much of his message content was what I would call foundational, as he ministered to many kids who were still "babes in Christ." Hearing teaching and preaching on that level was especially good for me as a new believer.

Youth chapel was held on Sunday evenings during choir practice, so Geri and I often heard four messages each Sunday—Sunday
school/adult Bible study, Sunday morning service, youth chapel,
and the Sunday evening service. What a spiritual feast every week! It
helped us shine our lights!

## The Call to Ministry

Our son Mick had already made a decision in his life that God
was directing him toward a preaching ministry of some sort, and
so he attended a special class for "preacher boys." The classes were
conducted by the youth pastor. The class took place at six o'clock
on Wednesdays, just prior to the Wednesday night service. So once
again, I was able to hear two messages every Wednesday. I was getting
spiritual "super food"!

One special class I remember well took place on a Wednesday
in May of 1983 during a revival meeting with Dr. Bill Hall. The
Preacher Boys met in the Fireside Room at Calvary Baptist Church
that night, as usual. I took Mick to the class, and he joined the other
dozen or so boys in the front row of chairs. I sat in the back that
evening like I usually did. When Dr. Hall was introduced, he made
some remarks to the young men, stating that he did not prepare anything to speak to them about; rather, they could ask questions of him
about the ministry.

When he asked for questions…crickets! No questions! The
silence was deafening and seemed to last forever! My anxiety level
raised for the boys, thinking, *Do not let the opportunity pass! Ask
something!* But there were no questions. Finally, from the back of
the room, I raised my hand, and when Dr. Hall acknowledged me, I
asked this question, "Dr. Hall, would you please tell the young people how they can know they are called to the ministry?" His response
was quick, and it was to the point. He said, "First, take an inventory
of the spiritual gifts God has given you. Then look at the desire He
has put in your heart. And finally, take a step of faith in surrender to
Him." *Kaboom! Wham! Zoiks!* Whatever other exclamation you can
imagine. That is what I felt immediately upon hearing this. And it

was like God saying, "Mike, I am talking to you! You are the one I am calling!"

Amazement! Surprise! A little shocked. *How could this be? I am not one of the Preacher Boys, I am a thirty-five-year-old businessman!* And then the fear began to arrive! If this was really happening, what would my wife think? What if I left my job for ministry? People would think I have gone crazy! How would we survive financially? It would be such a radical change!

The Preacher Boys class ended, and somewhat stunned, I made my way to the main auditorium for the evening service. I met Geri and the kids there in our usual place, second row on the left side of the main aisle. The service started. I could not begin to tell you what happened in that service that night. I was so preoccupied with the question, "What is Geri going to think about this? How bad could her reaction be?" The preaching ended, an invitation was given, and I stood there in stone silence until it was over.

I do not remember if it was on the way home or after we got home that I broke the news to Geri. I told her, "I think God is calling me into ministry." Her response floored me! She said, "I know that. The kids and I have been praying since you got saved that God would call you into the ministry." Somewhat confused and astonished, I replied, "What? Why didn't you tell me?" She said, "I wanted God to tell you!" How wise was that?

The next night in the revival meetings, at the invitation time, I stepped out to make the commitment known publicly, and the whole family went forward with me to share the moment. What a blessing that was!

As we stood at the front of the church auditorium, a number of people came up to rejoice with us. One person asked a question for which I was totally unprepared. They said, "Where are you going to go to college?" I responded, "For what?" They replied, "To prepare for the ministry." Honestly, that thought had never crossed my mind. Although I had been taking in a lot of preaching, it made sense that I would need some additional Bible knowledge and a more thorough understanding of ministry.

# Off to Bible College

Dr. Weniger had previously announced he would be leaving his position as pastor of Calvary Baptist Church early in the summer and assuming the president's role at Maranatha Baptist Bible College in Watertown, Wisconsin. After some discussion with him, we determined Maranatha would be a good place for us to get some additional training. And so we moved to Watertown that summer. Dr. Weniger, knowing my family well and understanding the needs of his new ministry, asked if I would like to work at the college as I went to school. It would be beneficial for me and to the college. And so I became the manager of the bookstore.

Life was radically different for our family when we made the move. We took an 80 percent cut in monthly compensation. We moved into an old farmhouse with a single bathroom. Geri started working with me at the bookstore, which was her first job outside the home since we started having children. That put an incredible strain on her.

Our daily schedule became frantic! Mick was in high school, Michelle in junior high, and Kelly in elementary school. Everyone's schedule was different and busy! I took a full load of classes and worked when not in class. Managing school events, church, and family time was chaotic at best. It seemed like we were being pulled and pushed in every direction. On top of that pressure, our house back in Normal, Illinois, was not selling and did not sell for an entire year. We ended up taking a significant financial loss to finally strike a deal with a buyer. That proved to be a real bank-draining test of faith for us!

# Cutting My Preaching Teeth

Dr. Weniger had told me that once we had gotten through our move to Watertown, I should start looking for preaching opportunities and check-in with the extension office at Maranatha to let them know I was available. Mr. Paul Stephens was the students' extension director. When I let him know of my desire, he told me to ask the youth pastor at our local church, Randy Tanis, to have me preach to the youth so Mr. Stephens could hear me. Randy was not keen on the idea, as he was brand-new to his position and did not want to give up the pulpit for this purpose. When I told Mr. Stephens, he said, "Okay, come to my office tomorrow afternoon and preach to my secretary and me." My thought, which I did not express aloud, was, "Are you kidding me? Preach to two people?" Well, I showed up the next afternoon and did my best to preach to him and his secretary. Awkward, for sure!

Apparently, I did not do too badly because the following Saturday, just a couple of weeks into my first year in school, Mr. Stephens came to me and asked a strange question. He said, "How would you like to fill the pulpit in Rochelle, Illinois, next Sunday?" My first thought was, *With what?* What did the pulpit need to have done to it? That response certainly showed my ignorance. What was really needed by the church in Rochelle was someone to do the preaching on Sunday, as they had recently lost their pastor. After being schooled by Mr. Stephens, I agreed to "fill the pulpit" and had a whole week to prepare a message for Sunday morning and another for Sunday evening.

Sunday came, and with a great deal of excitement, I got up early and got ready, got in my car for the two-hour trip to Rochelle, and hit the road alone. Geri and the kids would go to our regular service at Calvary Baptist in Watertown that day. I was praying and rejoicing the whole way as I thought over my messages. I was so excited and filled with gratitude.

Upon arrival, I was met by what I characterized then as "the two oldest deacons on the planet." After introductions, I asked, "What specifically would you like me to do this morning?" Their answer stunned me! They said, "Everything!" I responded with some anxiety in my voice, "What do you mean everything?" They said, "Everything! Welcome the people, open in prayer, make the announcements, lead the singing, and do the preaching." I thought to myself, *Lead the singing? Are you kidding me?* They had not heard me sing, and I was positive that once they heard me, they would change their minds about that part of my duties. However, they were steadfast in their request!

All the way from Watertown to Rochelle, I had thanked the Lord for the opportunity and told him I would do anything for him. I guess leading the singing was part of the "anything" I had promised to do for the Lord, but it was the furthest thing from my mind. And I was certain it was not one of my "gifts."

Well, I did as the old fellas requested. We had a wonderful morning with the folks there. I had lunch with a wonderful family. The evening service was good too. As I was ready to leave, they asked if I would come back the following week. I said, "I sure would." When I went back the next Sunday, I had another student come along with me. He was skilled and trained in song-leading! Jonathon and I would team up together for the next several months. From September 1983 until March 1984, I was the interim pastor of First Baptist Church of Rochelle, and Jonathon led the music.

In February of 1984, Dr. Weniger asked if I would be willing to travel with the Maranatha Chorale for their spring tour in late March. I would end up preaching twelve times in twelve churches in ten days on that tour. God richly blessed the concerts and promotion of the college, but more importantly, we saw seventeen people trust the Lord as Savior in those meetings, including the mother of one of the choir members. It was during this tour that God began to work on my heart and provide ministry direction. I began to think that doing itinerant evangelistic work would be my calling for the foreseeable future.

Some confirmation of this desire took place shortly after returning from our tour. Mrs. Thelma Cedarholm directed Maranatha's other large musical group, the Handbell Choir. Dr. B. Myron Cedarholm, the founder of Maranatha and President Emeritus, usually traveled with the choir and did the preaching. One day at school, Dr. Cedarholm came to me and asked if I would fill in for him and preach following the Handbell Choir's presentation on an upcoming Sunday evening service at a church in Jefferson, Wisconsin. He was going to a graduate's ordination counsel and service in another city and did not think he could be back in time. I was happy to accept the invitation.

That Sunday evening in Jefferson, the Handbell Choir did their program in a packed house. I arose and went to the pulpit to preach and had the people open their Bibles to my text. About that time, as I looked up, in the back door walked Dr. Cedarholm, and he sat down next to his wife. Too late to make a change of preachers now, and so I began preaching. We had a wonderful service. When we were finished and leaving the building, Dr. Cedarholm came to me and thanked me for filling in for him. Then he said some of the most encouraging words to me. He said in his own unique style, his head kind of bobbing back and forth, "Brother Duffy, you sounded just like Billy Sunday!" I was shocked. That was a high compliment, and it came from a genuine source. Dr. Cedarholm knew Billy Sunday, one of the finest evangelists in America during the early twentieth century. God had greatly used this man to reach thousands of souls with the Gospel of Jesus Christ.

After my first year of college was over and the summer passed by working in the office at Maranatha, now as the office manager, I was also asked to become the interim pastor at Bay City Baptist Church in Green Bay, Wisconsin. I will have more to say about that later in this book.

## My Call to Serve as an Evangelist

The fruitful choir tour and now an encouraging word from a seasoned minister of the Gospel. The ministry and office of the evangelist was now at the forefront of my mind and heart and would eventually be the life path that God would take me down.

One of the personal benefits of being an evangelist was that God took me deeper into the Word of God. I would be preaching nearly every day of the week and often multiple times a day. I needed to be well studied in order to be well prepared. As it is with most people who minister God's Word, their study ends up addressing many issues in their own life, resulting in both positive and negative conviction and, as a result, spiritual growth. They are more convinced about the right things and more repulsed by that which was not right in their own life.

And then, as one might expect, my ministry resulted in many coming to me with questions or the need for counseling at some level. Responding to questions about life-impacting issues is a big responsibility. Those asking already had a measure of confidence in you because they came to you and asked. They were not looking for my opinion, however; they were looking for God's instruction on the matter. That responsibility stimulated personal growth in my own life too. The principles of Scripture and their application to my own life helped my light to shine.

## A Life-Changing Moment

One day, while studying Jesus's Sermon on the Mount, God revealed to me one of my most life-changing moments. In Matthew 5:16, Jesus said his disciples were to "let your light so shine before men, that they may see your good works, and glorify your Father which is in heaven." The first thing I understood was that my life was like a light shining in a dark place. Others would see it; in fact, they would not be able to ignore it. If I was present, the light was there. I needed to be intentional about shining it. In other words, I needed to be careful about how I lived to keep it shining brightly. The second thing about the verse was this: my life was on display in the world in which I lived. Others would see my behavior. They would see what I do and where I go and hear what I say and so on. These two portions of the verse were fairly easy for me to understand.

But then there was this life-impacting part of the learning session. I began to understand that as people observed my life, they would form an opinion. The opinion was not to be about me; rather, it was to be about God. The word *glorify* carries the concept of "projecting an accurate opinion." As people watched me, my life should be projecting an accurate opinion of who Almighty God is! And those observing should form in their minds an accurate opinion of who He is and what He is like. It was not about my reputation or fame, but rather it was about God's reputation. If I were to live godly, then the attributes of God should shine through. On the one hand, this truth set me free from the intimidation others might bring. On the other hand, this was a great responsibility, helping others form a right opinion about God.

The Apostle Paul expressed this concept, too, as he was exhorting the church in Corinth when he said, "Now then we are ambassadors for Christ, as though God did beseech you by us: we pray you in Christ's stead, be ye reconciled to God" (2 Corinthians 5:20). Ambassadors, representatives in a foreign land—they represented the leadership of the country in which they were citizens. And now, since my citizenship is in heaven, it was clear who I should be representing with my life on planet Earth. (For more on this, see Philippians chapter 3.)

I later read a wonderful little book titled *Christ Esteem: Where the Search for Self-Esteem Ends*. It reinforced what I had already learned from the Bible. My identity is no longer in me but in Christ. What people think of Him because they watched me is more important to me than what they think of me. I want Christ's acceptance, not the acceptance or approval of man. You cannot even imagine how freeing this truth is until you truly embrace it! You are now free to serve anyone,' or should I say *everyone*! No encounter or conversation need be intimidating anymore.

## Are You Proud to Be an American?

Having asked for a raise of hands, this question set an audience up! I often asked the question as I began preaching a message about pride. Had I not studied the Bible, I, too, would have raised my hand in the affirmative. I would follow this up with another question: "How many of you are proud of your children or grandchildren?" Once again, there were many hands acknowledging they were proud of them!

These questions seemed like a good way to provide a wake-up call about the deceitfulness of sin. Because pride is a sin! And it seems to be a *root sin* that leads to many other, perhaps most, sins. Eventually, this sermon would be one of the most memorable and requested sermons I have ever preached.

What does God say about pride? In the KJV, we read the words, "pride, proud, proudly" 106 times. In their context, there is not one occasion where God puts His stamp of approval on pride. Not in any form or fashion! God is very clear in His Word when it comes to the issue of pride. Read these passages, and I think you will agree:

> *These six things doth the LORD hate: yea, seven are an abomination unto him:* (so repulsive that God wants to flee from our presence) *A proud look, a lying tongue, and hands that shed innocent blood, An heart that deviseth wicked imaginations, feet that be swift in running to mischief, A false witness that speaketh lies, and he that soweth discord among brethren.* (Proverbs 6:16-19 KJV)

> *The fear of the LORD is to hate evil: pride, and arrogancy, and the evil way, and the froward mouth, do I hate.* (Proverbs 8:13 KJV)

> *When pride cometh, then cometh shame: but with the lowly is wisdom.* (Proverbs 11:2 KJV)

> *Only by pride cometh contention: but with the well advised is wisdom.* (Proverbs 13:10 KJV) (It is the root cause of contention, not a symptom!)

> *Every one that is proud in heart is an abomination to the LORD: though hand join in hand, he shall not be unpunished.* (Proverbs 16:5 KJV)

> *An high look, and a proud heart, and the plowing of the wicked, is sin.* (Proverbs 21:4 KJV)

There it says it plainly—it is sin!

To demonstrate how deceitful sin can be, let me encourage you with this. Try substituting the word *thanks* or *thankful* for the word *proud* and see what happens.

"Thank God I am an American! I am thankful for my children and grandchildren and what they accomplish." Does it change who gets the credit? And this is the point of the deceit. Our role is to glorify God, not ourselves. When we are proud, we are robbing God of His glory! Being thankful gives Him the credit, and that glorifies Him.

This is one of the most profound, life-changing truths I discovered because I studied the Bible!

## The Pathway to Happiness

Another profound truth I learned was that the pathway to happiness in this life is through serving, not being served. As contrary as that might seem because of our cultural norms, it is the lesson that Jesus taught his close followers.

In John 13, the Lord Jesus Christ has just revealed to his disciples that he would soon depart this world and return to the Father in heaven. After finishing supper with his disciples, Jesus rose up, laid aside his own garments, took a towel, and girded himself. He prepared a basin of water and began to wash the feet of the disciples and dry them. This was a task that was usually delegated to the lowest servant in the house.

When Jesus got to Peter, Peter was repulsed by Jesus's action and declared, "Lord, dost thou wash my feet?" Jesus responded by telling Peter that although he did not understand this action now, he would understand it later. Peter, always quick with a response, right or wrong, declared emphatically, "Thou shalt never wash my feet!" Jesus quickly rebuked Peter by saying, "If I wash thee not, thou hast no part with me." Peter, understanding his error, told the Lord to wash not only his feet but his entire person.

When Jesus completed washing the feet of the disciples, he sat down and asked, "Do you know what I have done to you?" He went on to explain that their master had just washed their feet, and now they needed to learn to wash one another's feet. This was an example of what their mindset should be—the mindset of a servant!

Jesus then taught them the principle behind the illustration. The servant is not greater than the master, and he as the sent one was not greater than the one who sent him.

So having given them the visual illustration for an example and instructing them with the timeless principle, Jesus made this statement: "If you know these things, happy are you if you do them." How profound! The pathway to happiness is through serving! Not just knowing it but doing it! And I can attest to the truth that this is the pathway to happiness in this life!

By the way, this does not apply only in church but also in every area of life. Servant leadership is not a man-made strategy for success in business or other endeavors. It is God's strategy for those he has sent out into the world with the most important message ever conveyed to man, the Gospel of Jesus Christ. As the Master's servants, they are to be a shining light in a world of darkness!

## Active Church Participation

From the earliest days of my faith journey, our family has belonged to a local church. Calvary Baptist Church in Normal was incredibly special to me as a new believer. I am still learning of the impact it has had on my life. And, as you may know, a church is not a building; it is people. The word used in the Bible, *ecclesia*, is a Greek word meaning, "the called-out ones." Today we talk about going to a church, and we are thinking about going to "a building." The building is really the place where the church gathers or meets for services and events.

When we left Normal for Bible college, we joined a local church in Watertown. Calvary Baptist Church was their name also. Later, as we looked for opportunities to serve, we moved our membership to a recent church plant in Horicon, Wisconsin—Horicon Baptist Church. After college, it was back to Normal and reuniting with Calvary Baptist Church. After a few years, the Lord moved our family to Chetek, Wisconsin, for a ministry with Camp Chetek. While there, we were members of Faith Baptist Church in Chetek. A dozen years later, Maranatha called me to serve on their staff, and we reunited with Calvary Baptist in Watertown. And from Watertown, Geri and I moved our "empty nest" to Kentucky, joining Bluegrass Baptist Church where we serve today.

Being part of a local church—a church, by the way, that Jesus is building—is crucial to our purpose as Bible-believing Christians, followers, or disciples of Jesus Christ. As part of the family of God, we unite with other believers for fellowship and encouragement. The Lord gives us an under-shepherd who watches for our soul. We worship together and weep together as the family of God. We watch for and care for each other. We are instructed in the Word of God and the ways of God. According to Ephesians chapter 4, it is the place where God will stabilize us and mature us, preparing us to live in this world and minister to this world. Church is a place where we begin to understand the spiritual gifts God has given us to exercise, and then it provides an opportunity to put them to practice.

It is a place where we learn to love God and love others. While many look for what they can get out of the church, I learned early that I should be focusing on what I can contribute to the church, and to do so, I should be serving others. One can only imagine if every church member had this same viewpoint, how different and how much more effective their church would be.

## Study the Word

I love to study the Bible. In the early days of my Christian life, my study involved reading much about what others had learned in their studies. There are thousands of commentaries and books written from which we can glean spiritual understanding. However, the more mature I have become, the more limited, it seems, my toolbox has become. I can appreciate and respect what others have to say; however, conviction comes when the Holy Spirit convinces me of the truth of God's Word. What the Word says is everything!

Just reading the Bible is an amazing process. Getting a morning appetizer or thought to begin a day of meditation in personal devotions is good too. Doing Word studies or character studies also has its place and can be quite beneficial. I really enjoy these processes. As a maturing Christian, I have enjoyed book studies or concept studies too. Recently I completed a study and preached a series of messages from the Gospel of Matthew I called "Establishing the Patterns." The concept was, "What patterns were established by Jesus in his early, earthly ministry?" The following are the titles and texts of those lessons:

- Message #1—CONTEXT—"Jesus Begins His Earthly Ministry" (Matthew 1)
- Message #2—PROCESS—"Help Me!" (Matthew 4)
- Message #3—MOTIVATION—"The Happiness of Hope and the Hope of Happiness" (Matthew 5:1–12)
- Message #4—PURPOSE—"An Exalted People with and Exalted Purpose" (Matthew 5:13–16)
- Message #5—UNDERSTANDING—"Religion or Relationship?" (Matthew 5:17–48)
- Message #6—WARNING—"The Private Nature of our Relationship with God" (Matthew 6:1–18)
- Message #7—PRIORITY—"Perspective Determines Priorities" (Matthew 6:19–34)
- Message #8—ENCOURAGEMENT—"Avoid Distraction, Stay Focused" (Matthew 7:1–20)
- Message #9—CONFIDENCE—"How Stable Is Your Foundation?" (Matthew 7:21–29)
- Message #10—REFLECTION—"Getting from Here to There—Redemption to the Great Commission" (Matthew 28:16–20)

You might find this outline helpful as you look at those early chapters of Matthew too. I expect you will get something else, and even more than this, as you invest time understanding these rich passages. Enjoy the journey!

## Comfort in Trials

Another way I learned to shine the light and to grow personally is found in 2 Corinthians 1:1–7.

> *Paul, an apostle of Jesus Christ by the will of God, and Timothy out brother, unto the church of God which is at Corinth, with all the saints which are in all Achaia: Grace be to you and peace from God our Father, and from the Lord Jesus Christ. Blessed be God, even the Father of our Lord Jesus Christ, the Father of mercies, and the God of all comfort; Who comforteth us in all our tribulation, that we may be able to comfort them which are in any trouble, by the comfort wherewith we ourselves are comforted of God. For as the sufferings of Christ abound in us, so our consolation also aboundeth by Christ. And whether we be afflicted, it is for your consolation and salvation, which is effectual in the enduring of the same sufferings which we also suffer: or whether we be comforted, it is for your consolation and salvation. And our hope of you is stedfast, knowing, that as ye are partakers of the sufferings, so shall ye be also of the consolation.* (2 Corinthians 1:1–7)

From time to time, all of us go through trials and troubles. Suffering is a normal part of the Christian life. And if we are blessed, someone comes alongside us and comforts and encourages us. It might be in times of sickness or the death of a loved one. It could be a financial situation you are facing. Perhaps a relationship has gone south and is in trouble. Many are the possibilities here.

When these times come and the comfort and care is given, it usually makes a significant impact on the one being comforted. A great need is being met. Help is close by when you are feeling the most helpless. The intellect and emotions of those being comforted are deeply affected. Understanding, gratitude, and appreciation seem to happen with a different level of intensity during these times. Genuine love is expressed and received.

I have gone through some tough times in my life. To some degree, I have experienced poverty, shattered relationships, the horrors of war, physical illness and injury, death of loved ones, failures in business, heartbreak from progeny, and the list could go on for a good while. During many of these situations, I have been the recipient of much comfort. And it is during these times of being comforted that I was also learning how to comfort others. That is God's plan. It is part of the purpose of the suffering he ordained for us. It is during times like this that our lights shine.

## Is He the Easter Bunny or Santa Claus?

An observation I have made in life is this: Because men do not recognize the "works" of God and they do not know the Word of God, they have no relationship with God. He is no more real to them than the Easter Bunny or Santa Claus.

I believe the remedy for this condition is rather simple: Read and study the Bible. It is the account of God's historical work with mankind in the past, it describes his present work, and it reveals some of His working plan for the future. "Faith comes by hearing, and hearing by the Word of God!" (Romans 10:17).

Nearly two thousand years ago, the Apostle Paul wrote to the believers in Rome about this same issue. He said, "For whatsoever things were written aforetime were written for our learning, that we through patience and comfort of the scriptures might have hope" (Romans 15:4). In Paul's day, he was telling the people to look back to the Old Testament scriptures to see how God worked in the lives of people back then, people like Joseph, Moses, David, Esther, Isaiah, and others, and that would teach the Romans how God was working in their lives today because God does not change.

When man sees God's work and understands God's Word, then that man will come to know that God has a will for him and wants to be in a vibrant relationship with him.

# Mercy, Grace, Love, and Peace

To simply summarize what I think "shining the light" looks like for a believer, I think it would include the following: cooperating in God's process of change by willingly putting off or putting away the ungodly things in our life of which we become aware. By actively seeking to know the will of God through study of and meditating on His Word. By happily obeying and embracing the things we are learning that God wants us to do. Living faithfully to God and His Word with the desire to project an accurate opinion of who God is. Intentionally using the gifts and opportunities God gives us to share Christ with others.

This is only possible because of what God has done in my life. In a recent personal study, I focused on four words that in some ways sum up the whole of my life and, for that matter, the life every believer can have. These words are mercy, grace, love, and peace.

*Mercy*

I define this word as God holding back the judgment I deserve. Anyone who understands who God is and who they are, if they were honest with themselves, would not want what they deserve in God's economy. I quickly learned in this study that we cannot begin to appreciate mercy until we understand our own sinfulness. But there is another word we need to understand, too, and that is *wrath*. What I have earned for my sin is the wrath of God. And there are plenty of examples of the wrath of God in the Bible. We tend to think of only the cataclysmic—the flood, Sodom and Gomorrah, the Apocalypse, etc.—but the truth is, all sin, and all kinds of sin, is judged.

Mercy is more than compassion. It is *active* compassion. The act of mercy brings an easing or ending to the suffering, pain, or judgment one is experiencing or expecting.

The good news is this, the Bible teaches us that "God is rich in mercy..." (Ephesians 2:4).

Perhaps our best response to God's mercy should be humility, gratitude, and being merciful to others in order to glorify God.

*Grace*

I love the word *grace*. This passage that the Apostle Paul wrote to Pastor Titus is especially precious to me:

> *For the grace of God that bringeth salvation hath appeared to all men, Teaching us that, denying ungodliness and worldly lusts, we should live soberly, righteously, and godly, in this present world; Looking for that blessed hope, and the glorious appearing of the great God and our Saviour Jesus Christ; Who gave himself for, that he might redeem us from all iniquity, and purify unto himself a peculiar people, zealous of good works.* (Titus 2:11–14)

To me, the word *grace* is best understood as "enablement." I am saved by grace through faith. I was completely unable to do anything to remedy my lost condition. As a guilty sinner before God, I was condemned. The trial was over, "For all have sinned, and come short of the glory of God" (Romans 3:23). The judgment had been determined! "The wages of sin is death" (Romans 6:23). But through Christ's sinless sacrifice of his own life on the cross, shedding his own blood for the remission of my sin, and his resurrection, I was enabled, able to respond to God's drawing, and believe. My faith in Christ's finished work reconciled me to the Father.

I love how the Apostle Paul spoke of God's grace to the churches of Galatia. "I am crucified with Christ: nevertheless I live; yet not I, but Christ liveth in me: and the life which I now live in the flesh I live by the faith [moral conviction] of the Son of God, who loved me, and gave himself for me. I do not frustrate [nullify, or set aside] the grace of God: for if righteousness come by the law, then Christ is dead in vain" (Galatians 2:20–21). To claim to live the Christian life and trust that your goodness and good works will be sufficient to get you to heaven frustrates the grace of God; it is the rejection of his love and enablement in favor of your own ability!

Some define grace as God's unmerited favor toward man. It certainly is that. Some have used the acrostic GRACE to define grace:

**G**—God's
**R**—Riches
**A**—At
**C**—Christ's
**E**—Expense

Perhaps one of the all-time favorite hymns ever written and still sung on a regular basis in many churches is "Amazing Grace." It says a lot about this grace:

> Amazing grace how sweet the sound
> That saved a wretch like me
> I once was lost, but now I am found
> Was blind but now I see
>
> 'Twas grace that taught my heart to fear
> And grace my fears relieved
> How precious did that grace appear
> The hour I first believed
>
> Through many dangers, toils, and snares
> I have already come
> This grace that brought me safe thus far
> And grace will lead me home
>
> When we have been here ten thousand years
> Bright, shining as the sun
> We've no less days to sing God's praise
> Than when we first begun

We will not fully appreciate the grace of God until we acknowledge and accept our own inability! I love this verse written by Jeremiah the prophet: "O Lord, I know that the way of man is not in himself:

it is not in man that walketh to direct his steps" (Jeremiah 10:23). The simple truth here is this: the capacity for me to direct or control my own life just does not exist! It is not in me! Oh, how I need the grace of God! Growing in the grace and knowledge of the Lord Jesus is one of my highest priorities in life!

*Love*

Perhaps the most quoted verse in the Bible is John 3:16. It says, "For God so loved the world, that he gave his only begotten Son, that whosoever believeth in him should not perish, but have everlasting life" (John 3:16).

It is almost inconceivable to understand how God, in His holiness and righteousness, could love a sinful man like me! But to comprehend why He would send his only begotten Son to die for me? No words for me to explain this!

The love that is expressed in this verse is an "unconditional love." And perhaps that is all the explanation we need. His love is unconditional. If there were conditions, we would be in real trouble.

Consider Paul's writing to the church at Ephesus:

> *But God, who is rich in mercy, FOR HIS GREAT LOVE WHEREWITH HE LOVED US, Even when we were dead in sins, hath quickened us together with Christ, (by grace ye are saved); And hath raised us up together, and made us sit together in heavenly places in Christ Jesus: That in the ages to come he might shew the exceeding riches of his grace in his kindness toward us through Christ Jesus. For by grace are ye saved through faith; and that not of yourselves: it is the gift of God: Not of works, lest any man should boast.* (Ephesians 2:4–9)

It is God's love that motivated His mercy, holding back the wrath that we deserve. Perhaps a line from one of my favorite hymns is appropriate here: "Amazing love! how can it be—That Thou, my

God, shouldst die for me?" God's love for us is a great love—abundant, unmerited, and amazing!

It seems to me that we all have a tendency to try and do something to make God love us even more. That would be an exercise in futility. He loves us, period! And His love for us is a great love! And because He loves you, just love Him back!

*Peace*

When I think of peace, I think of the peace *with* God and the peace *of* God. Perhaps this passage in Paul's letter to the church at Ephesus best describes the peace *with* God:

> *Wherefore remember, that ye being in time past Gentiles in the flesh, who are called Uncircumcision by that which is called the Circumcision in the flesh made by hands; That at that time ye were without Christ, being aliens from the commonwealth of Israel, and strangers from the covenants of promise, having no hope, and without God in the world: But now in Christ Jesus ye who sometimes were far off are made nigh by the blood of Christ.*
>
> *For he is our peace, who hath made both one, and hath broken down the middle wall of partition between us; Having abolished in his flesh the enmity, even the law of commandments contained in ordinances; for to make in himself of twain one new man, so making peace; And that he might reconcile both unto God in one body by the cross, having slain the enmity thereby: And came and preached peace to you which were afar off, and to them that were nigh. For through him we both have access by one Spirit unto the Father.*
>
> *Now therefore ye are no more strangers and foreigners, but fellowcitizens with the saints, and of the household of God; And are built upon the*

*foundation of the apostles and prophets, Jesus Christ himself being the chief corner stone; In whom all the building fitly framed together groweth unto a holy temple in the Lord: In whom ye also are builded together for an habitation of God through the Spirit.*
(Ephesians 2:11–22)

Imagine this: aliens, Godless, living in a hostile world, and no hope! How much worse could it have been? And then a person, Jesus, became the peacemaker, reconciling us to our creator! He is our peace. Peace with God is through a person, not a program, not sacraments, not a religion, or organization. Not through our own wealth or our works! Peace with God is through Jesus and Jesus alone.

And once the peace has been made and we are reconciled to God, we are now a child of God, a joint heir with Jesus!

Because we are His and it is by Him all things consist, we can rest in His power and providence. He knows everything. He sees everything. He is never surprised! Our sins are forgiven. Our eternal destiny is settled, heaven with God forever! He will never leave us or forsake us! This is the peace *of* God in our lives. This is truly peace that passes understanding. I do not understand all of it! But I can experience His peace. Consider what Paul wrote:

*Be careful for nothing; but in everything by prayer and supplication with thanksgiving let your requests be made known unto God. And the peace of God, which passeth all understanding, shall keep your hearts and minds through Christ Jesus.*
(Philippians 4:6–7)

When these four words permeate your life, your light will truly shine. Your life will be that shining city on the hilltop. It will be like the beam of light from the lighthouse that stands on the rocky cliffs above the sea, warning the sailors on a stormy night of the impending danger as they near the shore.

As you live out these words, your life experience will be meaningful and joyful. You will be fulfilling God's purpose for your life. Let that light of yours shine!

# Grandpa Shared the Light

*And I thank Christ Jesus our Lord, who hath enabled me, for that he counted me faithful, putting me into the ministry; who was before a blasphemer, and a persecutor, and injurious: but I obtained mercy, because I did it ignorantly in unbelief.* (1 Timothy 1:12–13)

Grandpa shared the light by telling others of the Good News of the Gospel so they would have the opportunity to be saved.

My opportunities to share the Gospel and the work of God in my life have been many. I took to heart the Apostle Peter's exhortation: "But sanctify the Lord God in your hearts: and be ready always to give an answer to every man that asketh you a reason of the hope that is in you with meekness and fear: Having a good conscience; that, whereas they speak evil of you, as of evildoers, they may be ashamed that falsely accuse your good conversation in Christ" (1 Peter 3:15–16).

I also have taken to heart Christ's great commission, "And he said unto them, Go ye into all the world, and preach the gospel to every creature" (Mark 16:15). This verse also has a special meaning to me because of some circumstance at church the first year I was saved. Pastor Weniger had arranged for a special New Year's Eve watch service that year. Different individuals and families would come to the platform and sing or share something relevant to the season. Our kids sang. I was with them, not to sing, however, but to quote a memorized verse of Scripture. It was Mark 16:15. Even as a new believer, this verse and its content were at the forefront of my heart.

Here are some of the opportunities where I had to "share the Light":

- *My baptism*

    For several consecutive weeks, one of the church members at Calvary, Max Foster, taught new believers some of the basics of the Christian life. This class was extremely helpful in the early days of my relationship with Christ. It helped me understand the new context of my life as a child of God. It is here that I learned the real purpose of baptism.

    It is somewhat humorous now to recall some of the conflict I had in my mind as I considered baptism. One of the first conflicts was this: I had been baptized in a Catholic church in my first week of life. I really did not remember that happening, as you might imagine, but I had a certificate stating that I was baptized. Obviously, that was not *believer's* baptism. I did not believe anything at that age.

    Another conflict was this: I was concerned about what others would think as they saw me standing in the baptismal tank. Typical peer pressure! After all, I was a grown man, thirty-one years old. But then, is that not the point of baptism? It is a public declaration of your identity with the death, burial, and resurrection of Jesus Christ. You want others to know! I was publicly declaring that I had put my faith in Christ, having believed the Gospel, and now I wanted to share that with the world.

- *Visitation*

    Calvary Baptist Church in Normal, Illinois, was an independent, evangelistic Baptist church. They were enthusiastic about taking the Gospel to the community. There was an organized plan to reach the community with the Gospel by going out on Thursday evenings into the community and following up on people who had recently visited the church or simply making a "cold call" by knocking on the door of a home and attempting to share Christ with whoever answered the door. As part of this program, during the early portion of the Wednesday evening service, Pastor Ken Barth, our assistant pastor, would say, "Anyone who was going on visitation this week, raise a hand." They would receive a piece of paper on which they were to put their name and then drop it on the offering plate when it was passed. Someone at church would match the names of those who are going out on visitation and send someone with experience with a novice, and they would supply them with information for them to make a couple of follow-up calls on people who had recently visited the church or made some sort of inquiry. Week after week, I heard Pastor Ken go through the same routine. Finally, out of curiosity and with my ignorance, I went to Pastor Ken after one of the services and said, "Could I ask you a question?" Consenting, he said, "Sure." I then asked, "Are there a lot of people dying around here?" Puzzled, he responded, "Why do you ask that?" I said, "Well, you have announced visitation each of the last several weeks." To me, visitation was when you went to the funeral home to comfort someone who had lost a loved one! Knowing I was a new believer, Pastor Ken did all he could to conceal his amused response. Once he explained what visitation was, I was more than happy to participate in the initiative.

Week after week, on Thursday nights, I would go into the community and share the Gospel with people I thought needed to hear the good news. It typically involved going with another person who was more experienced than I. I made some wonderful friends as we worked together in this ministry.

At first, I was very nervous going out to share the Gospel. I knew that my Bible knowledge was extremely limited, and I was afraid someone would ask me a question for which I would not have an answer. Fear is paralyzing sometimes. It keeps you from doing what you know you should do.

One night, I shared this fear with a guy named Wayne Carpenter. His response to me was so impactful. He said, "You will always have an answer to any question that may be asked of you." My response was, "Really, how so?" He said, "Your answer can always be, 'I do not know the answer to your question, but I will try and find out. I will plan to come back next time to share the answer with you.'" Not only was that a good answer, but it was also a good strategy. It left the door open for another conversation.

One thing I learned is that a very high percentage of people had no idea what the Bible said or if heaven was in their future. Of course, when asked, most people would say they wanted to go to heaven, even though they had little or no concept of what it would be like. It was the opposite of hell, and that was good enough for them.

When burdened about sharing the Gospel with someone, I like to kindly ask them first if I could ask them a personal question. If they consent, I ask this follow-up question: "If you got up to the gates of heaven today and the Lord met you outside the gates and said, 'Why should I let you into heaven?' what would you tell him?" You see, that question cannot be answered with a simple yes or no answer. If they answer the question, they will be telling you what it is in which they are trusting to get to heaven. For example, if one says, "I am keeping the Ten Commandments," you know they are trusting in their effort to keep them, even though they cannot keep them all the time. If they say, "I am doing the best I can," you know they are trusting in good works. This gives you a place to begin your conversation about salvation.

• *Work relationships*

It was a real test of my faith to share the Gospel with my coworkers. After all, they knew me, the old me! I had engaged in the same behaviors that I now identified as being sinful. I had to be careful not to come across as judgmental, and I did need to acknowledge my own sin too. After all, that is what God was saving me from.

My life patterns were changing too. It had been typical that after a sales meeting in the office or wherever we were meeting, we had to head to the local bar for happy hour. I could no longer be comfortable doing that. On one occasion, we were in a hotel conference room in St. Louis for a meeting. When the meeting ended, most of the guys headed for the bar. I headed for my hotel room. Some time passed, and there was a knock at my door. It was one of the salesmen from our company. His name was Jeff. He asked why I did not come to the bar. I shared with him my decision to follow Christ and shared the Gospel with Him. He was respectful but did not commit himself. After he left my room, I remembered Jeff is a Jewish man. I wondered if he would ever believe.

One of the most challenging shares in my early Christian life was with an executive of a company who was one of my best customers. We became friends, and on many Saturday mornings, we would go golfing together. It was common for him to bring a half gallon of orange juice and a quart of vodka. We played and drank together. After my conversion, we continued our Saturday morning golf encounters but only for a short time. When I did not participate in the drinking, my friend wondered why, so I told him I had put my trust in Christ and felt it was no longer a good practice for me. He began to lose interest in my participation. Before long, we were no longer golfing together.

Perhaps one of the most dramatic shares was with my former boss, Tim. Tim had been my boss for a few years. We had known each other for about a decade. In fact, when

I was in management in Omaha, near our corporate office, I helped train Tim when our company hired him.

On this occasion, I had been working as a salesman for Tim, who was the division manager of the St. Louis region, in which my sales territory was located. I had just resigned my position, giving significant notice so they could replace me before I went off to Bible College to train for ministry. Tim called and asked why I was resigning. I shared my testimony of salvation and the work God had been doing in my heart about ministry. Then Tim floored me by saying, "You know I'm a Christian. In fact, I studied for the ministry too." Shocked and without thinking, I said, "Tim, why didn't you tell me about Christ?" Absolute silence on the other end of the phone line! How sad. I often wonder about the shame Tim must have felt at that moment for not sharing the Gospel with me or with the others whom he led. It was a great life lesson for me.

My resignation afforded me another opportunity to share. My most significant customer was the State Farm Insurance Company. I had developed a wonderful relationship with their home office. They were by far my biggest customer, too, and they were an especially important customer companywide. That resulted in our vice president of sales, John O'Brien, making a trip from the corporate office to see me a couple days after I submitted my resignation. John and I knew each other, having been together at many company functions. When he arrived in Bloomington-Normal, I picked him up at the airport. He immediately asked again why I was leaving. I shared with him, like I did with Tim, that God had been working in my life and I was headed for full-time vocational ministry. His reply was, "I am not surprised!" Those words were both comforting and confirming to me.

- *Preaching the Gospel*
  Writing to a church that had a lot of problems, the Apostle Paul wrote:

> *For the preaching of the cross is to them that perish foolishness; but unto us which are saved it is the power of God. For it is written, I will destroy the wisdom of the wise, and will bring to nothing the understanding of the prudent. Where is the wise? where is the scribe? where is the disputer of this world? hath not God made foolish the wisdom of this world? For after that in the wisdom of God the world by wisdom knew not God, it pleased God by the foolishness of preaching to save them that believe.* (1 Corinthians 1:18–21)

It has been the great privilege of my life to be a preacher of the Gospel of Jesus Christ. It is by the calling of God, and of no merit of my own, that I have had this wonderful ministry. I have recognized my calling to be the office of the evangelist, which Paul wrote of in Ephesians 4:11 and likened unto that of Phillip that Luke recorded in Acts 8 and who is also mentioned again in Acts 21:8. (See also Acts 6:1–4 as Phillip was one of the seven.)

Some of my early preaching included a few messages at the Home Sweet Home Rescue Mission in Bloomington, Illinois. I went there with my son, Mick, who also preached there.

Our youth leader, Pastor Tim, also had me preach two messages one summer at Castle Rock Camp in Montana on the senior high youth group trip. That trip remains a very special memory to me to this day. A young lady named Trina was saved during one of the services I preached. What a tremendous blessing it was for me to see God work in this fashion. God used the unskilled preaching of a relatively new believer to save a soul! How special is that? What a God!

I remember that morning having risen early to prepare my heart, I went to the banks of the West Gallatin
River that flowed through the camp and sat down to read
my Bible. As I sat there, I noticed in the shallow water three
stones lying in a cluster. Each was about the size of the palm
of my hand. One stone was black, one was white, and in
between them was a red rock in the shape of a heart. My
mind immediately went to the words of "wordless book"
presentation of the Gospel: "My heart was black with sin,
until the Savior came in. His precious blood I know, has
washed me white as snow." I reached down and picked the
stones out of the cold rushing water. They are in my curio
cabinet to this day as a reminder of the work and grace of
God in my life during that time.

- *Interim pastoring*
  In a previous section, I mentioned my ministry as an
interim pastor in Rochelle, Illinois. That opportunity to
preach Christ was also an opportunity to "cut my preaching teeth." In addition to my work at the college and my
classwork, I now had the responsibility of preparing two
messages a week. This was certainly a new experience for
me. Not much free time in those days!
  As my second year of college started, I was asked to
fill the pulpit at Bay City Baptist Church in Green Bay,
Wisconsin. This church was a little more than a two-hour
drive north of where we lived in Watertown. After that first
Sunday, the church leaders asked me to be the interim pastor. That was confirmation that my preaching was at least
tolerable! I ended up being the interim pastor the entire
school year. On the last weekend of college, the church wel-
comed their new pastor, Maurice Bender.
  Bay City was a special blessing to me and to my family. All of us went up to Green Bay most weekends. We
would spend the Sunday afternoons at the homes of different families in the church, and so we met a lot of peo-

ple who became good friends. God blessed our ministry there. We saw people saved, baptized some, and watched a church heal and thrive. We would return to Bay City on several occasions, including five different weeks for revival and evangelistic meetings.

* *Mike Duffy Evangelistic Association, Inc. (a 501(C)3, a not-for-profit corporation)*

   After finishing my second school year, having received the training I had gone to Maranatha for, our family moved back to Normal, Illinois. At the recommendation of some, I formed the corporation and began my ministry of itinerant evangelism. That first summer, we did a few vacation Bible schools and Christian camps. I would attend preachers' meetings whenever possible. I had prepared a little brochure about my ministry, and it had some endorsements on it. In addition to Dr. Weniger's recommendation, an endorsement from Evangelist Rom Comfort was especially important. As word got out, my preaching calendar began to fill up for the fall. It was quite full from September through November of 1985. That was a real blessing and, as I look back on it now, a quick start for an evangelist. The calendar for the next year was being booked too.

   I had no meetings in December and January scheduled, and so I took a job with a contractor in our church, who was building a house. I did construction work for two months and then hit the road again, preaching revival and evangelistic meetings. My calendar for the rest of 1986 and beyond quickly filled up, so I did not have to engage in secular work after that first winter.

   Through the years, I have had the privilege of preaching in many weeklong meetings in churches. It was common to teach and preach three times on Sunday and once each night Monday through Friday for these meetings. Sometimes the emphasis was on revival, other times on evangelism. It seemed like each week took on its own unique character. I guess that should not surprise us, as God knows the hearts and needs of His people. There were also times when I think the meeting was more focused on helping or encouraging the pastor. That was a good thing, as being a pastor is difficult work and often goes without praise or acknowledgment.

- *Christian camps*
  - Planting of a seed for Christian camping
    Although our family had experienced family camp at the Bill Rice Ranch in the summer of 1980, there was a seed planted in my heart during my family's first exposure to Camp Chetek. During the summer of 1984, our family attended a week of family camp there. It was a refreshing break following my first year of Bible college. The preaching and fellowship were great that week. Pastor Collins Glen was the keynote speaker, and the missionary was John Raehl, a missionary to Brazil. We enjoyed a lot of the activities that were available to the campers, and we were fed well!

    The accommodations for our family, however, were "less than stellar." We were split up into two "open-air" rooms above the dining hall. My wife, Geri, and our two girls were in one room, and my son, Mick, and I were across the hall in another room. We used the shower house in a building next to the dining hall. This was quite different from the comforts of our home we were used to. The week did produce some good memories, though. We met some new friends and were challenged and encouraged by the preaching and teaching of God's Word.

    One humorous experience we still talk about happened as we got ready for bed one night. As we began to settle into our rooms, there was a bat flying through the rafters of that long old building back and forth over each of the fifteen or so "open-air" rooms.

Screams would begin at one end of the building and cascade to the other end as the bat flew back and forth. Mick and I could hear my wife and daughters as the bat flew over their room. We thought it was hilarious until the bat took a dive toward Mick's face. He screamed and quickly pulled his sleeping bag over his head to protect himself!

While we were both laughing, something stirred my mischievous nature, and I tossed a pair of rolled-up black socks over the walls into the girl's room! There was a loud scream and then a thunderous crash as Kelly jumped from the top bunk down to her mother's bed. To say the least, not everyone was amused! Eventually, the bat flew down the staircase, and the episode ended.

My first impressions of Camp Chetek from that week were mixed. I thought the concept of Christian camping was impressive; however, the facilities there were old and not well kept. And when I looked back at our experience, I thought there were a lot of missed opportunities, perhaps because of lack of organization and a "this is how we've always done it" mindset. I found myself thinking or saying, "What if?" over and over. I say this not to be critical but to point out that little did I realize then God was beginning to form a burden in my heart and shaping a vision of what was to come. A seed had been planted.

God was also using another experience in a camp ministry as He formulated His plan for our future. I was the speaker for seven consecutive weeks at Camp Assurance in Georgetown, Illinois. Speaking in camps had already become a regular part of my itinerant ministry. We spent the most part of each summer at Christian camps. That summer at Camp Assurance, we had weeks for both junior-aged kids and teens. During a couple of the weeks, there was a particular volunteer worker who came from Eagledale Baptist Church in Indianapolis, not only transporting kids but also serving as a camp counselor. He brought kids from inner-city Indianapolis to camp at his own expense in his big white Cadillac. I came to understand that this man, a single man who was an attorney by profession, did this every summer. What a neat ministry and what wonderful stewardship of his talents and treasures! His example and story impacted my heart! A seed was clearly planted by this experience.

- Our call to Camp Chetek

During the winter of 1989, I had been on a mission trip to what was then the USSR—Russia and Ukraine specifically. Perestroika (restructuring) and Glastnost (openness) were in full swing bringing major change to that nation. It was an amazing time! We transported nearly twenty thousand Bibles into those countries and had wonderful opportunities to preach the Gospel of Jesus Christ multiple times every day. Our trip included ministries in four major cities—Leningrad, Kiev, Lvov, and Moscow. Thrilling times, for sure. We preached in the streets, the town squares, the subways, some universities and schools, and some government buildings. The hunger for the truth was incredible! Upon returning to America, we immediately began planning to return in the summer of 1991. However, God's plans were different than ours.

As we approached our expected departure date in mid-August of 1991, we got news that the Russian travel agency had "made an error" in scheduling our group. We were told we were not scheduled for 1991 but rather a year later, in the summer of 1992. At least that was the story they told us. How that impacted us was this: my family and I now had a large void on our travel calendar. Our next scheduled meeting was not until late September at Greendale, Wisconsin.

My wife and I decided that since the calendar had opened up, we would take advantage of the time for some spiritual refreshing, and so we decided to attend the annual meetings of the Wisconsin Fellowship of Baptist Churches, which was being held that fall in Viroqua, Wisconsin. It would be a good time to hear some preaching and to fellowship with friends in the ministry with whom we had served and served with.

As the first session of that meeting was about to start, Pastor Glen Teasdale, who was seated directly in front of us with his wife, turned around and asked me if I would consider directing the ministry of Camp Chetek while basing our ministry of itinerant evangelism out of Chetek. Although this came as a complete surprise to me, the ministry at Camp Chetek had been in my heart and mind often since our initial experience there. All the what-if questions had been coming back to my mind occasionally. We spoke later that day and agreed to meet with the board of directors of Camp Chetek in just a few weeks while we were holding evangelistic meetings at First Baptist Church in Hillsdale, Wisconsin. This was just a few miles from Chetek. The week following the WFBC meeting in Viroqua, we had a series of revival/evangelistic meetings in Greendale, Wisconsin, not too far from Waukesha, Wisconsin, where Pastor Teasdale pastored a church. And so Pastor Teasdale and I met during the week to discuss the possibility further in preparation for the board meeting. At the board meeting, the leadership extended a call to me to serve as the director of the camp. In spite of some absurdities in this meeting, which I will leave out of this book, I accepted the call. I was now the camp director of Camp Chetek. God's plan was taking shape!

When news of the leadership change at Camp Chetek got out, one of the men that had been on the trip to Russia and Ukraine with us, Evangelist Tom Farrell, called me and invited me to attend the staff training in May at The Wilds, a large Christian camping ministry in South Carolina. Tom participated in this camp and their staff training time regularly. This would prove to be a big boost to our ministry at Camp Chetek. I used what I learned at the Wilds to create a staff training program for Camp Chetek.

Learning how to assemble summer staff and prepare them for summer camp ministry was a critical element in preparing us to minister to campers each year.

One of the unique things about Christian camping is that kids come apart from the influences of the world, get intensive exposure to God's Word, and are in the presence of many examples of godly people serving the Lord. This makes for a conducive environment for spiritual growth. Making sure the camp staff understood this and were on the same page was important.

I sometimes wondered about the motivation of some parents who sent their children to camp. Was it spiritual growth and decision-making that drove them? Did they just want their child to engage in fun activities? Or, perhaps, it was to just get the kids out of their hair for several days during the summer. One cannot know the heart of another. We just rejoiced that the kids were at camp, and that gave them an opportunity to grow in the grace and knowledge of the Lord Jesus Christ.

During our tenure at Camp Chetek, the Lord gave us some incredible ideas for reaching kids with the Gospel, and that ended up bearing much fruit. Here are some of those ideas:

- *Erb Rural Bus Service*—John and Vicki Erb owned and operated the school buses for the

Chetek School District. They lived on the property of Camp Chetek, as Vicki also served as the secretary/administrative assistant for the ministry. During the summers, they would use their buses to get kids to camp. They had already been doing this for a number of years. They had regular stops along Interstate 94 designated from Milwaukee in the southeast corner of the state all the way to Chetek, which was located in the northwest part of Wisconsin. Parents would put kids on these buses at the designated locations on Monday morning and pick them up at the same location Saturday afternoon.

– *Weekly shopper newspapers*—The Lord gave us the idea of advertising in these weekly shopper-type papers that were sent through the mail or delivered by carriers. We developed a nice quarter-page advertisement, being open and honest about being a Christian camp with a chapel program included. Of course, we mentioned many of the activities in the ad too. Horseback riding, swimming, skiing, boating, and all the other activities did have quite an appeal.

As we began to pursue the newspapers to advertise, we experienced a great blessing. Many of the papers, understanding our effort, offered to run the ad at no cost or at a reduced cost. Some would run the ad for more weeks than we were intending to purchase. We appreciated all the exposure.

We were able to reach many kids who came from homes where there was no spiritual interest, no church exposure, and were out of the scope of our normal promotion. Ironically, we found out it was less expensive for the parents to send their kids to camp for the week than it was to send them to day care. That no doubt helped parents make the decision to send the kids to Camp Chetek. Having the bus transportation from key locations made this opportunity appealing to parents.

This initiative proved to be phenomenally successful with many kids putting their faith in Christ. We were also able to share contact information with local churches in the same areas from which the campers came so they could follow up with them and reach their families. It was good for many on multiple levels.

- Junior Missions Outreach Week—how it began

The Apostle Paul was writing to encourage the believers in Rome when he made this statement, "For whatsoever things were written aforetime were written for our learning, that we through patience and comfort of the scriptures might have hope" (Romans 15:4). What he was saying is this: when these believers looked back at the Old Testament and saw how God worked in the lives of the people then, it would help the Romans understand how God was working in their lives today, and that would result in hope.

When one has the benefit of hindsight, it is amazing to look back and see how God orchestrates His work and uses His people. That is what this section is about. In His time and with His patience, God moves to accomplish His will. Along the way, there are many circumstances and happenings that can only be recognized by looking back. Witnessing, remembering, and testifying of one's experience brings the picture of God's work into focus.

This is the story of the amazing work of God using ordinary people and the humble context of Christian camping for more than a quarter century to transform many lives for His glory. It is the story of how this unique ministry came to be. Now, as the former director of Camp Chetek and the founder of Junior Missions Outreach Week, I can now see more clearly how God used some unique experiences in my own life to plant the seed and provide the vision to bring to pass the wonderful ministry of reaching inner-city kids who had little or no exposure to the Gospel.

My experiences with other camps and now the new opportunity as the camp director to shape and expand the ministry at Camp Chetek created and supported the vision God was developing in my mind. We would call this new ministry Junior Missions Outreach Week. The name was quite intentional, and it was in line with our newly defined mission statement, which read, "Camp Chetek's purpose, as a fundamental Baptist ministry, is to glorify God by using the controlled environment of Christian camping to help churches of like faith and practice fulfill the great commission to evangelize the lost and make disciples of those who believe." We regularly promoted the camp by offering every camper HELP—**H**ope, **E**ncouragement, **L**eadership, and **P**urpose. So here is a deeper dive into our thinking regarding the name, which simply described the vision:

– *Junior*—Our effort would be toward junior-aged kids, typically third through sixth grades. This seemed like the most logical age group to focus on, as camp would likely be interesting to them, and they are young enough that we might make a significant life impact by providing an intensive dose of love and some solid biblical instruction. We described this target crowd as "inner-city, under-privileged, unchurched boys and girls, ages 9 to 12." Planting and watering are important Bible principles when it comes to Gospel work, and this looked like the perfect opportunity to do it. The interest and demand would make age a "flexible guideline" as brothers and sisters of kids in this age group, who were beyond these boundaries, often wanted to participate too. It would prove to be a delicate balance!

- **Missions** – This would truly be characterized as "mission" work, Great Commission work. We would engage others in accomplishing the work. We would need people with financial resources to provide the scholarship money so the ministry of Camp Chetek could sustain this effort. We would need volunteers to labor with us to minister to these kids and operate the program. It would take a good number of people to pull this off. The work would be labor-intensive, for sure! It would take an army of prayer-warriors holding this effort up before the throne of God. We anticipated spiritual warfare as this initiative certainly was invading some of the devil's strongholds!

- *Outreach*—We would engage inner-city church ministries to locate the kids who would receive the scholarships and then transport them to camp. These local churches would also follow up with the campers after the week was over to continue ministering to them and to reach the rest of their families. The camp was doing outreach by helping the local churches with their outreach. This was truly a representation of our mission statement.

- *Week*—This would be a dedicated week in the camp's schedule, usually the first week after staff training, so the team was "fresh and excited."

We would use a regular "camp week" on the calendar with kids coming in on Monday and leaving Saturday morning. And as our counselors and staff would come to find out, a week was quite enough! The work was exhausting in every way, physically, mentally, and spiritually.

- *Sharing the vision*
Vision casting is an important responsibility of leadership. On April 12, 1992, I began a week of evangelistic/ revival meetings in Gibraltar, Michigan, with Pastor Mark Buhr. We had been to this church two years earlier and had a good week of meetings then. After the Sunday morning service, my wife, our daughters, and I were invited to have dinner with the Buhr family. As we enjoyed dinner and fellowship, Pastor Buhr asked about our new ministry at Camp Chetek. One of the things I shared with him was our vision to help reach inner-city kids. Pastoring just a short drive downriver from Detroit, he understood the vision and was quite interested in the concept. He asked if I would share it with his congregation in the Sunday evening service that night, and so I did.

You never know who is in a crowd of people when you are speaking or preaching. And as any experienced preacher would know, you never know what God is going to accomplish in a service or with a message. That Sunday evening, there was a dear lady present listening intently as we shared the vision. She came to us later that week and shared her own story with us. She had lost her husband several months earlier, a godly man who loved the Lord. She told us how there were many gifts of money given at the funeral and that she had been praying regularly for God to show her how to use that money. It was $2,750! Sharing our vision provided her with the answer. This elderly widow handed us a check and said that God had answered her prayer, and she wanted to use the money to help us initiate the Junior

Missions Outreach Week. It was enough to fund twenty-five kids that first year, and the inner-city churches had no problem finding the willing souls to be part of that first week of camp. It has always amazed me that God would take the life of one of His servants and then use the occasion to provide the resources and to save many souls! That is how I viewed His provision, God taking the life of one to bring eternal life to many. What an amazing master planner God is!

In the early years of Junior Missions Outreach Week, we raised money by sharing the opportunity in a brochure that was widely distributed. In that brochure, there was a section titled "From the Camp Director and Founder of Junior Missions Outreach Week." It read as follows:

*I cannot think of a better way to invest God's money than by sponsoring a child to come to this week of camp. To get the Gospel to a child at an early age is very important. It does not take long for the "cares of the world and the deceitfulness of riches and the lusts of other things entering in" to "choke the Word" so that "it becometh unfruitful" (Mark 4:19).*

*There are so many distractions in life that keep people from dealing honestly with God about the salvation of their soul. It seems like the older one gets, the more distractions there are.*

*Please consider helping us sow the seed to a child in need!*

*Dr. Mike Duffy*

Our first year, we reached out to several churches in inner-city Minneapolis and Milwaukee. Three churches responded to our invitation to participate. Two of the churches expressed the immense value it was to their ministry and continued to bring campers every year. They were Gospel Light Baptist Church and Family Baptist Church, both in Minneapolis, both just a couple hours' drive from camp.

The first year of Junior Missions Outreach Week, we operated on a "traditional" Christian camp schedule for each day, including a chapel program in the morning and an evening service. We invited an itinerant evangelist, Stan Harris, to do the preaching. It was a learning experience, for sure.

Expecting to have kids with no church experience— and many with no personal discipline to speak of and little appetite for Bible preaching or teaching—to embrace this schedule proved to be a bad expectation. We had more occasions of chaos than I care to mention. A forty-minute sermon to kids of this background and this age just was not going to be the best approach.

A year or so earlier, I had been gathering all kinds of discipleship material from publishers and ministries so I could share these resources with pastors as we traveled and encourage them in the difficult work of disciple-making. One of the books I obtained was a discipleship curriculum from New Tribes Mission. It was called *Firm Foundations* by Trevor McIlwain. There were approximately fifty short lessons taking a person with no Bible experience from creation to Christ and the resurrection. I loved the concept, and we began a process to develop a curriculum that might prove more effective with these kids than our traditional camp schedule.

We wanted the teaching times to seem to the campers to be more impromptu. This prevented kids from anticipating the preaching and resisting or rebelling to distract from our program. We wanted to use many different venues as contexts for teaching. For example, we found a nice spot by the obstacle course in the woods, a great spot near the horse corrals, the waterfront steps, and many others where we would have the kids just stop, be seated, and listen to an eight- to twelve-minute message. It worked well for the groups we had! We could communicate effectively in a brief period of time and keep the kid's attention.

We wanted to use as many illustrations and object lessons as we could to help drive home the messages. Many of these kids struggle to learn academically but learn well through visuals and experience. One illustration of particular impact was the crucifixion. We had a staff member hanging from a large cross on the platform in the chapel, depicting the crucifixion of Jesus. We simply marched the kids past it in silence. A short time later, we would share with them the story of the crucifixion. It was powerful and it made a significant impact on the kids.

Our intent with the curriculum and the program was to start with a "clean slate" and introduce the kids to the God of heaven and His creation and then build their understanding sequentially, line upon line, precept upon precept. We learned a lot from our ministry to these kids that challenged our traditional molds. For example, just the concept of "God the Father" was a challenge to kids who came from a primarily matriarchal society where the concept of a father carried a negative connotation. How could the Father help me and meet my needs when a father has never been part of my life experience?

As we developed this twenty-three-message, chronological curriculum of Bible preaching and teaching, our hope was that by the end of the week, they had a good glimpse into the big picture of the Gospel and the kingdom of God that they understood their condition and position as a lost sinner, and they understood the hope of salvation that was only found in the forgiveness of sin by grace through faith in the finished work of Jesus Christ. Our staff and counseling team was on constant watch to help those under conviction invite Jesus into their lives as Lord and Savior.

Prior to bringing campers in for this special week, we spent a week of intensive training with our program and counseling staff. Many of them came from solid Christian homes and good churches. Their lives could be characterized as somewhat "sheltered." They lived with structure and accountability most of the time. However, it seemed no amount of training would be sufficient to prepare the young men and women for what was about to come as they spent their first week of summer camp with the campers of Junior Missions Outreach Week. It was culture shock, for sure! One could truly characterize this experience for them as eye-opening and heartbreaking. Many of the deep, life-changing spiritual decisions that would be made during Junior Missions Week would be by our staff, adults and college kids alike. It is interesting to look back now and see how, as we were hoping to impact them, they impacted us!

This past fall, with more than twenty-eight years having passed since the beginning of Junior Missions Outreach Week, Randy Tanis, the camp's current director, sent a video message to my son and me. It was a video of testimony from Randy's office from just a few days earlier by a man who had attended Junior Missions Week as a camper in one of the early years of this ministry. He shared how camp had changed his life. He is known to us affectionately as JK or Big John.

When JK arrived at Camp Chetek for the first time, the pastor that brought him shared with me how his mother had sold everything they had that week, including JK's clothes, to get money to support her drug habit. All JK had to his name was the clothes he was wearing. He had on a pair of shorts and a T-shirt that was in great need of laundering. He was wearing some ragged, size 11 gym shoes on his size 16 feet. JK was an exceptionally large young man!

My son's heart was broken for JK when he saw him, and so Mick headed for the Farm and Fleet store in Rice Lake to get JK some clothes. He knew they had a "big and tall" clothing section. He was able to find some multiple X's T-shirts and sweatpants there. Shoes, however, would be a bigger challenge. F&F did not carry shoes that large. Mick remembered that there was a Play-It-Again Sports store in Rice Lake, and they often carried gym shoes that had been acquired from NBA players who had shoe contracts with manufacturers. He arrived at the store and was able to find a pair of Nike basketball shoes, size 16, with the Nike swish! They were orange and white! Back at camp, Mick gave the clothes and shoes to JK. He was overwhelmed with this act of love and kindness. It made an enormous impact on his life. And he was especially happy with the shoes! Today, JK is serving the Lord and regularly brings kids to Camp Chetek. He loves the camp, and those who continue to make an impact on kids.

When I consider how God planted the seeds in my heart and arranged circumstance after circumstance using many of His people in many locations, I can only say, "What an amazing plan!" God's ways are not our ways! He is the master orchestrator! And Junior Missions Outreach Week at Camp Chetek is one shining example of His masterful work! Praise the Lord! And thank you, Lord, for allowing us to have a part in your wonderful work.

- *Preaching in camps*

    This became an important part of my ministry too. I loved this part of my ministry, as it impacted young people. Some of the camps I have preached at include Camp Ironwood in California; Camp Assurance and Camp Manitoumi in Illinois; Living Waters Farm in Bonaparte, Iowa; Amazing Grace Baptist Camp in Ottawa, Kansas; Camp Co-Be-Ac in Michigan; Castle Rock in Montana; the Wilds in North Carolina; Camp Calvary in Pennsylvania; the Bill Rice Ranch in Murfreesboro, Tennessee, and Flagstaff, Arizona; Rapidan Baptist Camp, Virginia; Camp Chetek, Camp Joy, and Northland in Wisconsin; Red Cliff

Bible Camp in Pinedale, Wyoming; and others operated by local churches at various locations.

- *Christian education institutions*

  My preaching ministry also included many Bible colleges, universities, seminaries, and Christian schools. These included Ambassador Baptist College, Lattimore, North Carolina; Bob Jones University, Greenville, South Carolina; Baptist College of Ministry, Menomonee Falls, Wisconsin; Calvary Seminary, Lansdale, Pennsylvania; Clearwater Christian College in Clearwater, Florida; Faith Baptist Bible College in Ankeny, Iowa; Faith Way Baptist College, Ypsilanti, Michigan; Indiana Baptist College, Greenwood, Indiana; Maranatha Baptist University in Watertown, Wisconsin; Northland Baptist Bible College in Dunbar, Wisconsin; Pensacola Christian College, Pensacola, Florida; Pillsbury Baptist Bible College in Owatonna, Minnesota; and scores of Christian schools.

  I enjoyed preaching in chapel for Christian schools. Most of the time, the environment was such that preaching was easy and enjoyable. It is wonderful to preach the truth to those whose heart is open to it. On some occasions, however, I would find myself in a chapel where the kids seemed cold and distant. Perhaps so familiar with the things of God that apathy had set in. That certainly is a real condition in which all believers must be careful not to find themselves.

  I remember well a chapel session at Bethany Christian Academy at Bethany Baptist Church in Galesburg, Illinois. I was at the church preaching a revival meeting for the week. During the daytime, I had the opportunity to preach in chapel for the academy. About midweek, as one chapel session was coming to a close, I gave an invitation for folks to respond to the leading of God in their hearts. It seemed as though the floodgates of heaven opened. One by one, the kids came forward in repentance or for prayer and some of the teachers too. With no additional pleading, that invi-

tation went on for well over an hour. There was a genuine revival taking place in the hearts of the student body,
faculty, and staff. It was a tremendous blessing to be part
of that special time. One never knows where or when an
outpouring like that will take place.

- *Bible Tracts, Inc.*

    Dr. Paul Levin founded Bible Tracts, Inc., a minis-
try of Bible tract printing and free distribution of those
tracts, and a radio broadcast called *Bible Tract Echoes.* The
program aired across America on many radio stations. It
was a fifteen-minute broadcast of preaching and testimony
of God's work through the tract ministry. Dr. Paul was a
member of Calvary Baptist Church in Normal, Illinois. He
was often on the road preaching, but his wife, Dorothy,
was at church faithfully. Their home was located in nearby
Carlock, Illinois.

    Dr. Levin was aging and needed someone to come
alongside him to, as he put it, "bring the ministry into the
twentieth century!" Some folks told us that Dr. Paul had
attempted to get someone to help, but Dorothy always
seemed to veto his selection. I do not know how true that
is, however.

    In any case, there was a unique situation that took
place one Sunday that demonstrates how the Lord uses "little things" to accomplish His will. Our family was planning
to attend family camp at the Bill Rice Ranch during the
upcoming summer. Dr. Paul spent his summers preaching
at the camp. Dorothy mentioned to my wife and me in the
foyer after one church service how she wished she could go
to the ranch too. I said, "Why don't you come with us?"
She declined, saying that they had a little dog at home she
needed to care for. I said, "Well, you can bring the dog
along with us!" She replied, "Really, you would let me do
that?" and we said we certainly would.

Dorothy did not go with us that summer; however, she was thrilled with the idea when Dr. Paul wanted to bring me on board, and so I became the director of Bible Tracts, Inc. Amazing how the Lord uses little moments like this!

As I continued my itinerant preaching ministry, from a distance, I was able to consolidate all the operations of Bible Tracts into one office at Calvary Baptist Church in Normal. We hired a staff, computerized the processes, and greatly improved the response time for shipping orders. The ministry thrived.

One aspect of the ministry that was not so appealing to me at this time was the radio broadcasts. I just had a difficult time going into a studio alone and preaching to a crowd of "no one"! It was just me in there, recording a message that would be delivered at some time in the future across the radio waves. It just was not my cup of tea.

It had taken a couple of years to accomplish the modernizing of Bible Tracts. I was not interested, however, in just being a studio preacher, and so I asked Dr. Levin to find someone who would become the new director.

• *Russia and Ukraine*

During one summer in the late 1980s, I attended the Remove Not the Ancient Landmarks conference at Ambassador Baptist College. Many preachers would attend this conference. During one of the morning sessions, Dr. Don Sisk was sharing his experience in Eastern Europe. He had just returned from a very fruitful trip to Romania. Romania was just then opening up to the Gospel. The people there were hungry for the truth.

I was sitting next to a friend, Evangelist Tom Farrell, during Dr. Sisk's session. As the session drew to a close, Tom and I turned to each other and said at the same time, "We need to go to Russia!" It seemed like a window of opportunity was opening, too, for preaching the Gospel and getting Bibles into that country. When the session was over, we were dismissed to a prepared lunch. Tom and I sat at a table with two other evangelists, Neil Cadwell and Billy Crockett. Before lunch was over, we had all agreed on a plan to take Bibles to Russia and preach a time or two if the opportunity arose.

Tom made contact with a missionary who had made some trips into the former Soviet Union and also had a radio program that had been broadcast to the entire country. Sam Slobodian and his father, Peter Slobodian, had a ministry called Baptist International Evangelistic Ministries, BIEM, based in a suburb of Chicago. Sam's wife, Amy, and Peter's wife, Mary, were both actively engaged in the ministry with their husbands.

Before long, the plan was finalized. We would have to travel as tourists, and as such, the Soviet government required us to visit some sites. We would go to these places in the mornings and then break away from our tour group for the rest of the day. We would take as many Bibles as we could carry with us and ship as many as we could ahead of our trip in a container. We would all raise funds to purchase the Bibles in the Russian language. I would also provide through Bible Tracts, Inc. the New Birth tracts that we had recently translated into the Russian language.

We opened the opportunity up to some pastors and laymen to go with us. The three evangelists plus myself, the three people from BIEM—Sam, Peter, Mary—seven pastors, and five laymen all made the trip. We planned to go for eighteen days. We would first arrive in Leningrad, sometimes in history called St. Petersburg. We would travel from there to Kiev and then Lvov, both in Ukraine. We would finish up our trip by going to Moscow.

We agreed that everyone in our team would pack lightly, carrying only one change of clothing for the whole trip and only necessary personal items. That way we could maximize the amount of literature we could carry with us. Each person would be able to take two suitcases and a carry-on bag. They would also have two cases of Bibles that were taped together with a handle for carrying the parcel. In addition to the Bibles, our group also took in several sets of Bible study help books that would be a real blessing to any pastor. We were able to ship nearly twenty thousand Bibles in a container ahead of our trip. We also raised a significant amount of cash and took it with us to distribute to some of the pastors and churches who were in great need. I am not sure how much money we took in total, but it was significant—tens of thousands of dollars. I personally wore a money belt that contained several thousand dollars.

While I could spend days writing about this trip, let me just touch on a few highlights from each of the locations we traveled to.

- *Leningrad*—While in Leningrad, our tour group went to two places of great significance, Catherine the Great's Winter Palace and the Hermitage Museum in Leningrad. The Winter Palace was the official residence of Russian emperors and empresses from 1732 to 1917, when the monarchy was abolished in the Bolshevik Revolution. Catherine died at the palace, aged sixty-seven, in 1796.

It was also the location where the thousand-day siege of Leningrad took place in World War II. Leningrad was a strategic prize on the Nazi plan. For nearly a thousand days, the Russian troops held off the Germans, eventually defeating them and liberating Leningrad. We saw the photographs of the devastation of the palace. But then, in contrast, we toured the palace after they repaired or rebuilt it and saw the lavish décor. I remember being amazed by the amount of gold on the fixtures, the walls, and the furniture.

The second place in Leningrad our tour group went was the world-famous Hermitage Museum. The treasures on display there were incredible. In one area was the world's largest collection of original Rembrandt paintings.

The *Sacrifice of Isaac* is a 1635 autograph oil on canvas work by Rembrandt, now in the Hermitage Museum. (Wikipedia)

As our group stood before this painting, the tour guide told us it was a picture of something totally unrelated to the Bible. Using our interpreter, Tom Farrell told the guide what the picture was really about and ended up leading the guide to Christ right there in front of the display. It was incredible to witness!

While our mission for this trip was to take Bibles into these countries, as preachers, our desire was also to preach the Gospel. We would all later share that our individual hopes were to preach at least once on the trip. But God is so good! All the preachers, and even the laymen in our group, all preached the first full day we were in Leningrad, and some of us multiple times than first day.

On that first Sunday morning, Pastor Pat Kappenman and I were taken to an unregistered church that met in an old Russian Orthodox church building. The church would provide a translator for us. Neither of us had ever preached through an interpreter before, but we did receive some guidance from those in our group who had. There were several hundred people in attendance, which was the first surprise. I preached a simple Gospel message from Romans 5, "No Condemnation." Upon giving an invitation to receive Christ as Savior at the end of my message, scores of people responded. It was a stunning moment for me. Then Pastor Kappenman preached, and the result was similar. We serve an amazing God!

When we were finally reunited with our group early in the afternoon, we found out everyone had preached, and many were saved in those morning meetings. While eating lunch, someone came in and asked if a couple of our men would be willing to go preach at the University of Leningrad. Tom and one of the pastors went and, once again, to a fruitful result.

Our group was emboldened. After our tour the next day, we met with a group of pastors from unregistered churches and then another group from registered churches. They knew Dr. Slobodian from his radio broadcast. These meetings were amazing, as we discovered a lot about what church was like for the people there. Some groups met in homes, some in the woods, others in abandoned buildings. Many of the pastors had been in prison for preaching the truth. In one of the meetings, we met with Peter Peters, considered the number two person in leadership of the unregistered churches in all of the Soviet Union, for more than three hours. It was stirring to hear the stories of faith in the midst of severe persecution.

· *Kiev*—After a few days in Leningrad, we traveled to Kiev, Ukraine. We were required to go on the morning tours, which were very interesting. We visited a very ornate Russian Orthodox church in Kiev, and we toured much of the city, which is known for its period-specific architecture in different areas. We visited a supermarket in Kiev while we were there. Only a handful of items were for sale. It was not even close to what we call a supermarket or even a convenience store. We are so blessed in America.

After our morning tours, we met again with groups of pastors. We learned about the restrictions the government had put on registered churches. It was challenging to hear how many were imprisoned for their faith because they obeyed God rather than man, or should we say the mandates of the government. We met with one pastor who informed us that there were three groups of churches, not just the two, registered and unregistered, as we had thought. The third group was the "autonomous registered church." In doctrine and practice, they were more like us than the other two. Pastors from all three groups shared testimonies of being imprisoned in the Russian Gulags.

The pastors were encouraged by our presence and wanted our group to do some evangelistic preaching in the city so they could observe. We went to the streets of Kiev. It was December, and so it was cold! Very cold. In fact, it was about twenty-five below zero outside and dark most of the day. The decision was quickly made to move inside, into the Subway stations, to do our work.

In the station, we found ourselves on one side of the tracks where people who were all going the same direction would congregate. Sam Slobodian took out his trumpet and began playing it. He was an extremely accomplished trumpeter. The uplifting music echoed through the corridors. It did not take long before we were surrounded by a huge crowd of listeners. The Russian people love music. Evangelist Neil Cadwell stepped forward after Sam finished and preached a simple Gospel message and gave an invitation. The response was incredible once again! Scores of people responded, and the Russian pastors who were with us got busy dealing with these repentant souls.

Our group made its way to the other side of the station, for those going the opposite direction, and once again, Sam played. Just like before, in short order, we had a huge crowd around us. I stepped out this time and preached a short Gospel message and gave an invitation. Once again, scores of people responded. I thought to myself, this must have been what the Apostle Paul experienced as he went from place to place preaching, and the Holy Spirit had gone before, preparing the way, and now empowering the Word as it went out to those who may have never heard before. Just incredible! Sharing the light in Kiev was amazing, truly amazing!

- *Lvov*—Lvov is the major city in Western Ukraine. Having the experience we had in Kiev, our team was anxious to get to preaching in Lvov. However, we were also required to be on the tours during the mornings there. Somewhere on our tour, we were in a park setting high on a hill, overlooking most of the city. We noticed that nearly every rooftop had these strange-looking antennas. We asked about them and were surprised to find out their purpose. It was not to receive radio or TV broadcasts. In fact, just the opposite. It was to scramble the broadcasts from Radio Free Europe. The communists did not want the people to learn anything about the freedoms the West had to offer. How sad! My thought was this: the Communist's control and power came by using deceit and lies. This is a life lesson we all need to remember.

Late one afternoon, our group piled out of our bus at the town center. It was beautiful, the opera house at one end of a park that was a few city blocks long. At the other end of the park was a place where the newspaper, *Pravda*, was posted.

By the way, here is what Wikipedia has to say about *Pravda*: "As the names of the main Communist newspaper and the main Soviet newspaper, *Pravda* and *Izvestia*, meant 'the truth' and 'the news' respectively, a popular saying was, "There's no news in Pravda and no truth in Izvestia." This ought to cause us to be careful about the news we hear. Is it truth, or is it propaganda?

In this park, there were several garden areas bordered by low brick walls. We watched the people topple a huge statue of Lenin in one of these gardens—very symbolic of what was happening. Once again, we had fruitful preaching sessions in this park. Literally hundreds of Ukrainians responded to our invitations to be saved. We had many pastors with us who did the follow-up work with these folks.

At another location, we opened a case of our New Birth Tracts that we had translated into the Russian language. As we stepped off the bus, people scurried to us and willingly took the material. When we had exhausted our supply, we got back on the bus. As the bus pulled away, I looked back and saw many people standing there reading the message of the Gospel. The light was being shared in Lvov.

We met during the evenings with some of the churches in Lvov. Many of those saved during the day were there to acknowledge their newfound faith. We had the pastors pass out the Bibles we had brought with us. I remember one elderly lady in particular. Upon receiving it, she clutched it like a mother would hold her newborn baby. She began kissing the Bible over and over. She was in tears, rejoicing, and so were we!

I remember, too, an incredibly special time the four of us evangelists had in Lvov. We were staying in a hotel and had gathered together in one of our rooms for a prayer meeting. We were all broken for the people, overwhelmed by the outpouring of mercy and grace from God we were witnessing at every turn. So much freedom to preach! So many willing to listen, starving for the truth. We were all experiencing what appeared to us an unusual moving of God's Spirit. Our response was one of great humility and awe! We prayed for a long time.

It was during this prayer time that God laid on the heart of Neil Cadwell to start a ministry that would become the Slavic Baptist Institute, a Bible college located at the Grace Baptist Church in Khmelinsky, Ukraine.

God was also doing a work in Sam's heart on this trip. BIEM has on their website today the following narrative:

In 1990 dramatic changes came to the ministry of BIEM with the advent of glasnost and perestroika in the Soviet Union. The collapse of Communism resulted in many new opportunities for ministry in Russia and led Sam and Amy to consider moving there. Discussing the matter with BIEM's board and with others with longtime involvement with the Slobodians and BIEM, both in Russia and the West, helped Sam conclude that they would be most effective operating from the United States. Today Sam serves as president of BIEM, and Amy works in the ministry's office. BIEM specializes in Russia and Eastern Europe, where the mission has planted numerous churches by supporting, training, and equipping nationals. BIEM also distributes Bibles and Gospel literature; maintains a seminary in Kyiv, Ukraine; translates and prints discipleship and pastoral training materials; conducts evangelistic outreach ministries; sponsors Christian summer camps for children and youth; provides material aid; and helps new congregations to build churches.

It was such a privilege to be part of the beginning of this amazing work. On the second trip I made with the Slobodians, I was able to conduct seminars for pastors, interview missionary candidates that BIEM could support or recommend, and do some preaching.

- *Moscow*—Moscow was the last stop on our trip. Once again, we met with pastors from the various groups and preached in many places. Our tours in the morning took us to some incredible places. We visited Red Square. At the center of Red Square is a parade ground where the government often displays their military might. There are other significant places bordering the parade grounds, including Lenin's Tomb, St Basil's Cathedral, and the Armoury in the Kremlin. This was somewhat intimidating as it is the epicenter of Communism in the world.

Visiting Lenin's Tomb was interesting to me. We waited in long lines to go into this heavily guarded room where the embalmed body of Lenin was on display.

What was interesting to me is, there seemed to be a "forced allegiance" the Soviet people were expected to give. Sad…and troubling! St. Basil's Cathedral is at one end of Red Square. It is beautiful and ornate. I was able to find a vendor selling hand-painted watercolor pictures of St. Basil's and purchased one that hangs in my office today. It is a constant reminder of the trip.

The Kremlin Armoury is one of the oldest museums of Moscow, located in the Moscow Kremlin, now a part of Moscow Kremlin Museums. The Kremlin Armoury originated as the royal arsenal in 1508 (Wikipedia).

There is a display of Fabergé eggs in the Kremlin Armoury. The most famous are his fifty-two "imperial" eggs, forty-six of which have survived, made for the Russian Tsars Alexander III and Nicholas II as Easter gifts for their wives and mothers. Fabergé eggs are worth millions of dollars and have become symbols of opulence.

There is a breathtaking display of coaches there too.

The Armoury is a fascinating museum.

My first trip to the Soviet Union was certainly a life-changing event for me. My love and appreciation for America grew exponentially. To see all the wealth and power in the government was an amazing contrast to how the people lived. Most were poor and lived in modest, cramped housing. It was told to us that the average women would spend as many hours a week in breadlines to get food for her family as her husband would spend working in a factory. One of the major cultural problems in the Soviet Union is alcoholism. It is no wonder to me depression runs high in the general population. I identify this as "the fruit of communism."

- *Ambassador Baptist College*
    Dr. Ron Comfort was a friend of mine. We met at a revival meeting where he was preaching in Normal. He and his team ate in our home on more than one occasion, and we spent some time together when he came to preach at Maranatha. As mentioned earlier in this book, Dr. Comfort gave my ministry a wonderful endorsement that I published in our ministry brochure. We spent time together at a couple of different Bible conferences too.
    Although I did not attend this particular meeting, I was aware that Ron had gathered many preachers in Indianapolis and announced his intent to start a college. The college's stated purpose was:

*Our mission is to do the best job possible both spiritually and academically to prepare men and women for ministry in Independent Baptist churches around the world.*

As one might imagine, the news was a blessing to some and a concern to others.
    He rented some property in Shelby, North Carolina, and started the school in 1989 with thirty-seven students.

The college relocated to its current location in Lattimore, North Carolina in 1997.

In the mid-1990s, Dr. Comfort had me preach the opening revival for the second semester of one of the school years. There were approximately 225 students at that time. I learned a great lesson in these meetings and got a wonderful blessing too. Let me share it with you.

I had been the director at Camp Chetek for a few years when I went in January to preach at this meeting. Our family was still quite dependent on our love offerings from our ministry of evangelism in churches, even though we had drastically reduced the number of meetings we would hold. I was not drawing any compensation from the camp at this time, although we spent the entire summer there. (That is a story I will save for another time!) The last day of August the previous year, I blew out my lower back. From August 31 until October 31, I was at home, unable to stand or sit. I crawled around the house on my hands and knees. I had back surgery on October 31 and then took a couple of months to heal. It was a difficult time, for sure. What added to the difficulty is that we had no meetings that fall, which meant no love offerings! So from May all the way to the end of the year, eight months, no income!

The meeting at Ambassador would be my first since the previous May. In the first service of the meeting, before I was introduced and got up to preach, Dr. Comfort came to the pulpit, asked the students to turn to a passage in the Bible, and then taught them a lesson about financial stewardship. He then floored me with this statement, "I am praying that the offering this week will be the largest love offering Brother Duffy has ever received." I thought to myself, *Are you crazy?* The audience was Bible college students, many of whom struggled to get into or stay in college! And to top that, this is the second semester of the school year! Just after Christmas! How could he expect them to give the largest offering we had ever received? He did not even know what our largest offering had been! He prayed, and the offering plates were passed!

Every service he followed the same pattern and made similar statements. There were four morning chapel sessions and five evening services. On Friday night, his statement again took me by surprise. He said regarding the offering, "We are almost there!" I thought, *Where? How does he know?* He prayed and passed the offering plates. We had a wonderful closing meeting that night. Sometime after the meeting, Dr. Comfort gave me an envelope with a check inside. I just put it in my Bible.

I had an early morning flight out of Charlotte the next morning. As I recall, it left at six in the morning for Minneapolis. I would arrive in Minneapolis, get my car, and then make the two-hour drive just in time for our Camp Chetek board meeting that afternoon. Very early the next morning, a new friend I made that week, Gary Norris, drove the college van to the airport, and two students studying for the ministry rode along. One of the students was Dwight Smith, who now has a wonderful ministry in evangelism. When we got to the airport, I was in a hurry to get checked in. The three men shook my hand and said some kind words. Dwight handed me a *Classic Soul Winners New Testament*, which I slipped into my jacket pocket, and we parted ways.

Once on the plane, as we began to taxi to the runway, I opened the New Testament and found these words written in the fly leaf:

*To Brother Duffy,*

*All week during the offering, I have had nothing to give and have been disappointed. Tonight, during the offering, I was praying about what God would have me give you, and the Lord laid this on my heart.*

*I hope and pray that you will use this for the Lord's glory to win many souls to Christ. Your ministry has been a blessing to my life and I praise God for it.*
*I love you and will be praying for you.*
*God bless you.*

*Dwight M. Smith*
*Col. 1:18*

My heart was full, but at that moment, it melted! How kind and precious! Then I took out the envelope from Dr. Comfort. When I looked at the check, I just started crying. It was the largest love offering I had ever received! My faith was greatly challenged in that moment. Why should I be surprised? Dr. Comfort had challenged the students with God's Word. He prayed to the God who owns the cattle on a thousand hills. In fact, he owns the hills too. Everything is His!

A stewardess stopped at my seat and asked if I was okay. I looked at her and shook my head yes. I had such a lump in my throat I could not say or do anything more than that. I cried all the way to Minneapolis.

When I reached my car in the parking garage, my mind turned to the board meeting. One element of the meeting was to be a discussion about the budget. Up to that point in the camp's history, offerings taken during the camp services were used for stuff. Shingles, new fences, repairing old used equipment, or whatever the most urgent need was. It was never to be a love offering for the man of God that was there to minister to us. I determined as I drove that this practice was going to change, and it was going to change now.

I made my pitch to the board that afternoon, and that day we had a new policy at the camp. We would budget travel expenses and an honorarium for each speaker, but then we would also take a love offering from the campers so they had an opportunity to be a blessing to the preachers. Everything the campers gave in the offering went to the preacher. This made a huge difference in our care for the men of God who ministered at the camp. I remember John Goetsch bringing a check back to me, suggesting someone made a mistake. The check was much larger than what he was accustomed to receiving at Christian camps. No mistake, however, just a blessing!

Several years later, in recognition of my work in the ministry, Dr. Comfort awarded me with an Honorary Doctor of Divinity degree from Ambassador.

- *Duffy's Myrtledale*
  You are likely aware that Duffy's was a treatment center for alcohol and drug addiction. My dad built the programs around the principles of Alcoholics Anonymous. So you might wonder, how does sharing the light come into play there?

  I spent a lot of time at Duffy's from 2008 through 2015. The financial crash of 2008 prompted my brother Gene to ask for my help. The business had taken a downturn and was headed for the first economic loss in its forty-year history. I was still serving at Eternal Vision but was able to set aside one week a month to travel to Myrtledale and see what I could do to stimulate the business.

  The more time I spent there, the more I could see some influence of God's Word in the programs of Alcoholics Anonymous. I began to research the origins of AA and was amazed to find out its roots were in Bible believing Christian efforts to win men to Christ who were suffering from alcoholism. As a result, their homes were shattering. It is worth sharing some of this history with you. Here are some of what I discovered:

  - The Washingtonian movement was a nineteenth-century fellowship founded on April 2, 1840, by six alcoholics (William Mitchell, David Hoss, Charles

94

Anderson, George Steer, Bill M'Curdy, and Tom Campbell) at Chase's Tavern on Liberty Street in Baltimore, Maryland. The idea was that by relying on each other, sharing their alcoholic experiences, and creating an atmosphere of conviviality (friendliness), they could keep each other sober. Total abstinence from alcohol was their goal. The group taught sobriety and preceded Alcoholics Anonymous by almost a century. Members sought out other "drunkards" (the term *alcoholic* had not yet been created) and told them about their experiences with alcohol abuse and how the society had helped them achieve sobriety (Wikipedia).

- The Oxford Group was a Christian organization founded by American Christian missionary Dr. Frank Buchman. Dr. Buchman believed that the root of all problems was the personal problems of fear and selfishness. Further, Dr. Buchman believed that the solution to living with fear and selfishness was to surrender one's life over to God's plan.

Buchman was an American Lutheran minister of Swiss descent who in 1908 had a conversion experience in a chapel in Keswick, England, where he attended a decisive sermon by Jessie Penn-Lewis in the course of the 1908 Keswick Convention. As a result of that experience, he would in 1921 found a movement called A First Century Christian Fellowship. By 1931, the fellowship had become known as the Oxford Group. The Oxford Group enjoyed wide popularity and success, particularly in the 1930s. In 1932, the archbishop of Canterbury, Cosmo Lang, in summing up a discussion of the Oxford Group with his diocesan bishops, said, "There is a gift here of which the church is manifestly in need." Two years later, William Temple, archbishop of York, paid tribute to the Oxford Group, which "are being used to demonstrate the power of God to change lives and give to personal witness its place in true discipleship."

In 1938, Buchman proclaimed a need for "moral re-armament," and that phrase became the movement's new name. Buchman headed MRA for twenty-three years until his death in 1961. In 2001, the movement was renamed Initiatives of Change.

The Oxford Group was incorporated in 1939. They developed, as a foundation for their work, four absolutes: honesty, unselfishness, love, and purity. They said, "Honesty is the eternal search for *truth*."

The four absolutes seem to have first appeared in a book by Robert E. Speer titled *The Principles of Jesus*. Speer laid down four principles (honesty, purity, unselfishness, love) that he believed represented the distilled, uncompromising, moral principles taught by Jesus.

The Oxford Group advocated *four practices* set out below:

- The sharing of our sins and temptations with another Christian
- Surrender our life past, present, and future into God's keeping and direction
- Restitution to all whom we have wronged directly or indirectly
- Listening for God's guidance and carrying it out

When Bill Wilson and Dr. Bob Smith set out to establish the tenets of AA, Anne Smith, Dr. Bob's wife, who had been a member of the Oxford Group, did the secretarial work for them. It may have been her experience that brought the biblical influence to the organizational table. Together they established the following original six principles (used by Bill W. prior to writing the Big Book):

1. Admitted hopeless
2. Got honest with self
3. Got honest with another

4. Made amends
5. Helped other without demand
6. Prayed to God as you understand Him

One can also see the biblical influence in the five C's they used: confidence, confession, conviction, conversion, and continuance. These five C's were identified as the process of life-changing undertaken by the life-changer. This life-changing process became the basis for AA's twelve-step work and the format for the Big Book chapter titled "Working with Others."

- *Confidence*—The new person had to have confidence in you and know you would keep his secrets.
- *Confession*—This refers to honesty about the real state of a person's life.
- *Conviction*—This is the seriousness of his sin and the need to be free of it.
- *Conversion*—The process had to be the person's own free will in the decision to surrender to God.
- *Continuance*—You were responsible as a life-changer to help the new person become all that God wanted him to be. Only God could change a person, and the work of the life-changer had to be done under God's direction.

Alcoholics Anonymous has been recognized for decades as the most successful treatment program for addiction. Understanding its roots then, this should be no surprise.

When I began to understand the history of AA, it was as though God was emboldening me to share the Gospel more, which I began to do. It seemed like God had someone prepared for me to talk to about Christ on every trip I made. It was never difficult to get a conversation started that would lead to a presentation of the Gospel. Through my years of leadership at Duffy's, I saw many guests and some staff come to Christ. It was a great blessing.

- *Keeneland Racetrack/Thoroughbred Training Center*
  When my wife and I moved from Wisconsin to Kentucky, we purchased a home in Woodford County near the city of Versailles. This was the heart of horse country. The Bluegrass Region is often referred to as the epicenter of the equine world and rightfully so.

  According to the *Encyclopedia Britannica*, "The region contains Kentucky's best agricultural land and thus became the first area to be settled. It became known for its abundant bluegrass and became famous for breeding fine horses; the calcium-rich soil imparts its minerals to the grass and thence into the horses' bones. The region is located in all, or part of, several counties in Kentucky, including Anderson County, Bourbon County, Boyle County, Clark County, Fayette County, Franklin County, and Garrard County."

  One of our neighbors was the Winstar Farm, a world leader in the Thoroughbred industry in breeding, breaking, racing, and rehabilitation of racehorses. One day, I went to the farm to meet the people there. I was introduced to the president of the operation, Elliott Walden. We shared a little bit about each other. Elliott was also serving as the head of the Bluegrass Farms Chaplaincy, a division of the Race Track Chaplaincy of America, at that time.

  When Elliott found out my background in ministry and in the addiction treatment world, he said, "You could be a great blessing to the chaplain at Keeneland, Mike Powers." Mike had Parkinson's disease and had difficulty speaking and preaching, and his mobility was becoming more limited. I went over to Keeneland the next day and introduced myself. Mike and I "hit it off" immediately. We would end up serving together for three and a half years before his retirement.

I loved the work there. While I was still CEO of Duffy's, I was able to volunteer my mornings to the chaplaincy. My management team in California did not come to the office before noon my time, Eastern Standard Time. I loved being around the horses and the horsemen. I had been a groom and trainer in my teenage years for a major racing operation in Illinois, so horses were "in my blood."

I also became the "voice" of the chaplaincy at Keeneland, as Mike struggled when he spoke. I walked the barns each morning, speaking to trainers, grooms, and hot walkers, and sharing Christ with them. I shared a Bible devotion over the intercom that was broadcast live to the entire complex each morning. This was a wonderful opportunity to share the light.

Keeneland had race meets every April and October. During these meets, I had multiple opportunities to preach the Gospel. During the meets, I would preach to the jockey colony at noon five days a week. I would preach a service in the Track Kitchen for the backside workers on Thursday evenings. On Sundays, which was a race day, I would preach a morning service for the grandstand workers about ten fifteen. And then I would lead another service for the maintenance workers and gate crew at about eleven and then the jockeys at noon. Along with the morning devotion, we were "sharing the light" a lot!

- *The not-for-profits*
  It was my joy and privilege to start several not-for-profit organizations. In addition to the Mike Duffy Evangelistic Association, Inc., by God's grace, we were used to start:
  - Eternal Vision—*The purpose of Eternal Vision is to promote quality and excellence in ministry by teaching biblical stewardship and building ministry endowments.*
    While leading the ministry of Camp Chetek, I was able to realize that Christian camping ministries

were labor-intensive, but they were not revenue-intensive. You could never earn enough with fees to properly compensate those who were working in the ministry. Well, Christian education is much the same. As a result, the actual cost of Christian education is often borne on the backs of the faculty and staff, not on the parents who send their kids to the schools. That is not to say the parents do not pay anything. Far from that! They usually pay a hefty tuition fee. What we are saying, though, is that is not the entire cost of the education. We found that it was rare that a Christian school's compensation package for faculty was even 50 percent of what an equivalent educator received in public education.

In addition to understanding this truth, while I was at Maranatha, I created a financial stewardship seminar that we conducted in churches. While we were hopeful some people would appreciate the instruction and support Maranatha, its true purpose was to help prepare believers to give account of their stewardship at the judgment seat of Christ. It truly was a ministry of discipleship.

I learned a couple of valuable lessons doing the seminars. First, pastors avoided teaching about money like the plague. It was extremely uncomfortable for them to do so, and they certainly did not want to be perceived as being after people's money.

The second important lesson was this: there was a lot of money in churches that was not well positioned to advance the Kingdom of God.

So armed with this knowledge, we designed and launched Eternal Vision for the express purpose of teaching financial stewardship and building endowments to support ministry, particularly Christian education.

Matt Davis, who had been serving as one of the attorneys for the Christian Law Association, joined me as cofounder of Eternal Vision. Matt could come at the financial issues from a legal perspective and do estate planning as well.

We started EV in January of 2007, developing our processes and products and strategies. We were able to begin promoting and presenting them in late 2007. Several endowments were initiated and early funding secured. There was a lot of enthusiasm about this ministry. Then in the fall of 2008, the financial collapse happened in our country. Charitable giving dried up overnight.

Matt and I recognized the difficulties that lie ahead, and so we prepared the company to endure that rough road. We eliminated all the employees and closed the office in downtown Watertown. He would manage the endowments out of his law office and take a position offered to him as vice president of Maranatha. At some future time, Eternal Vision would be prepared to reconstitute their efforts and begin promoting the cause once again.

I took a role at our family business, initially as vice president but shortly thereafter as president of the company.

The ministry of Eternal Vision will remain relevant and highly needed until the Lord comes.

- *Gene Duffy Foundation*—Not long after assuming the role of president at Myrtledale, a number of different people approached me asking how they could help. What could they provide for us? That proved to be a tricky question. We were a for-profit company who had been profitable for its entire history. It would be awkward asking people to donate.

I did, however, realize the spirit and desire behind their ask. It would be a blessing for them to be able to help us fulfill our mission. With my background, it was easy to produce a solution. We could start a not-for-profit foundation to which people could donate. The foundation could then help those in need of financial help get assistance in their recovery journey. And so, we launched the Gene Duffy Foundation in honor of my dad's incredible work for more than a quarter century.

Through those early years, several donors came forth, and we were able to scholarship a good number of people into treatment and provide for educational costs for some who were training to be counselors in the industry.

- *My New Legacy Foundation*—As time went by, our burden and focus seemed to shift from treatment to prevention. We formed a new foundation, My New Legacy, to advance a newly defined mission.

PURPOSE

We exist because life is intended to be lived to the full. Even in the midst of adversity and challenge, humankind has the opportunity to thrive. Key to our thriving is the investment we make in each other through meaningful relationship. The most substantial work of the New Legacy Foundation centers on the development of tools and strategies that promote the establishment and nurture of healthy relationships and push back against the stuff that seeks to steal away the opportunity for life that is both fulfilling and fruitful.

Ideally, the construction of a solid social and emotional foundation starts early in life. But regardless of age or life stage, each day represents a new page full of new opportunities for change and relationship building. Life's difficulties become the capital from which investment in a brighter future can be made. Such hopeful prospects are why we exist.

We made the work of the Gene Duffy Foundation one of the initiatives within My New Legacy. Our initiatives included:

REWRITING FUTURES INITIATIVE
The flagship tool of the initiative is the Discovery Series, which gives children a license and a platform to tell their stories, to dream, and to leverage the challenges that life brings. The Discovery Series is a tool to help build solid social-emotional skills, nurture healthy relationships, and provide abuse prevention.

LEGACY TOOLS INITIATIVE
The Legacy Tools Initiative is focused on the development of tools and strategies to help adults of all ages and in all walks of life. The My Life My Legacy resource is the first in a collection of tools to help adults begin to shape a legacy of inspiration and success for the generations that will follow.

THE GENE DUFFY INITIATIVE
Resources for addiction and treatment.

# SUMMATION

As you can tell by reading the pages of this book, I have lived a rich, full life. It has been the joy of my life to share God's Word with so many. All told, I have had the privilege of preaching in nearly a thousand ministries and venues. In each of these ministries, I had plenty of opportunity to "share the light"! In some cases, we have seen people come to Christ for salvation. Others have been inspired to get serious about their faith and grow in the grace and knowledge of the Lord Jesus. We have seen some make life-changing decisions and leave their secular careers to serve in full-time vocational ministry. Every decision has been important, and they all carry eternal impact.

I can echo the thoughts of the Apostle John that he penned to well-beloved Gaius in the little book of 3 John. He wrote:

> *Beloved, I wish above all things that thou mayest prosper and be in health, even as thy soul prospereth. For I rejoiced greatly, when the brethren came and testified of the truth that is in thee, even as thou walkest in the truth. **I have no greater joy than to hear that my children walk in truth.** (3 John 1:2–4)*

To hear and see my children, grandchildren, and great-grand-children walk in truth brings an unspeakable joy to my heart. And to see or hear of those to whom we have ministered walking in truth is also a blessing and a thrill. This, to me, is the essence of true riches!

I am grateful to the Almighty God for His mercy, grace, and love in letting me "see the light" and letting me "shine the light" and letting me "share the light." And as I look forward to one day being in His presence, I admit that I am motivated daily by the prospect of one day hearing from Him say, "Well done, thou good and faithful servant!"

May God bless you and encourage you for the investment of time you have made reading this autobiography of my life.

# ABOUT THE AUTHOR

Dr. Mike Duffy and his wife of fifty-six years have three children together, twelve grandchildren, and four great-grandchildren. Mike's life experience is characterized by service, integrity, leadership, and accomplishment. He grew up in a home that was shattered by alcoholism when he was in elementary school. Overcoming this tragedy and trauma early in life, he has experienced productivity and success on many levels.

Mike is a combat veteran who served a tour in Vietnam with an infantry battalion of the United States Army's Eighty-Second Airborne Division. He learned early the value and reward of working hard and excelled in a corporate career for fourteen years in administrative management and sales, receiving international awards at each level for outstanding achievement and accomplishment. Mike received Jesus Christ as his personal Savior at age thirty-one and committed his life to Christian ministry at age thirty-five, ministering God's Word in nearly one thousand ministries nationally and internationally.

The following statement from Mike reveals his heart: "There is trauma and tragedy everywhere. I believe that everyone will face some adversity in life. How one responds to that adversity will greatly shape their future. People can be paralyzed, damaged, or destroyed when adversity comes, or they can use adversity as motivation for positive change. We cannot change the past, but we do not have to live there either. We must learn from the past, look toward the future, but live today. Although no one can go back and change their beginning, they can begin today to change their ending. This is what hope looks like. I love serving God and others and have found that this approach in life is the pathway to happiness.

Printed in the USA
CPSIA information can be obtained
at www.ICGtesting.com
LVHW090052131123
763661LV00070B/2981